I0828204

COLONEL STARBOTTLE'S CLIENT

and Other Stories

BRET HARTE

Colonel Starbottle's Client and Other Stories

Bret Harte

PO Box 2211
Fairfield, IA 52556
www.1stworldlibrary.com
First Edition

LCCN: 2007930720

Softcover ISBN: 978-1-4218-4799-3
Hardcover ISBN: 978-1-4218-4702-3
eBook ISBN: 978-1-4218-4896-9

1st World Library Literary Society

Giving Back to the World

"If you want to work on the core problem, it's early school literacy."

- James Barksdale, former CEO of Netscape

"No skill is more crucial to the future of a child, or to a democratic and prosperous society, than literacy."

- Los Angeles Times

"Literacy... means far more than learning how to read and write... The aim is to transmit... knowledge and promote social participation."

- UNESCO

"Literacy is not a luxury, it is a right and a responsibility. If our world is to meet the challenges of the twenty-first century we must harness the energy and creativity of all our citizens."

- President Bill Clinton

"Parents should be encouraged to read to their children, and teachers should be equipped with all available techniques for teaching literacy, so the varying needs and capacities of individual kids can be taken into account."

- Hugh Mackay

CONTENTS

COLONEL STARBOTTLE'S CLIENT

CHAPTER I

It may be remembered that it was the habit of that gallant "war-horse" of the Calaveras democracy, Colonel Starbottle, at the close of a political campaign, to return to his original profession of the Law. Perhaps it could not be called a peaceful retirement. The same fiery-tongued eloquence and full-breasted chivalry which had in turns thrilled and overawed freemen at the polls were no less fervid and embattled before a jury. Yet the Colonel was counsel for two or three pastoral Ditch companies and certain bucolic corporations, and although he managed to import into the simplest question of contract more or less abuse of opposing counsel, and occasionally mingled precedents of law with antecedents of his adversary, his legal victories were seldom complicated by bloodshed. He was only once shot at by a free-handed judge, and twice assaulted by an over-sensitive litigant. Nevertheless, it was thought merely prudent, while preparing the papers in the well known case of "The Arcadian Shepherds' Association of Tuolumne versus the Kedron Vine and Fig Tree Growers of Calaveras," that the Colonel should seek with a shotgun the seclusion of his partner's law office in the sylvan outskirts of Rough and Ready for that complete rest and serious preoccupation which Marysville could not afford.

It was an exceptionally hot day. The painted shingles of the plain wooden one-storied building in which the Colonel sat were warped and blistering in the direct rays of the fierce, untempered sun. The tin sign bearing the dazzling legend, "Starbottle and Bungstarter, Attorneys and Counselors," glowed with an insufferable light; the two pine-trees still left in the clearing around the house, ineffective as shade, seemed only to have absorbed the day-long heat through every scorched and crisp twig and fibre, to radiate it again with the pungent smell of a slowly smouldering fire; the air was motionless yet vibrating in the sunlight; on distant shallows the half-dried river was flashing and intolerable.

Seated in a wooden armchair before a table covered with books and papers, yet with that apparently haughty attitude towards it affected by gentlemen of abdominal fullness, Colonel Starbottle supported himself with one hand grasping the arm of his chair and the other vigorously plying a huge palm-leaf fan. He was perspiring freely. He had taken off his characteristic blue frock-coat, waistcoat, cravat, and collar, and, stripped only to his ruffled shirt and white drill trousers, presented the appearance from the opposite side of the table of having hastily risen to work in his nightgown. A glass with a thin sediment of sugar and lemon-peel remaining in it stood near his elbow. Suddenly a black shadow fell on the staring, uncarpeted hall. It was that of a stranger who had just entered from the noiseless dust of the deserted road. The Colonel cast a rapid glance at his sword-cane, which lay on the table.

But the stranger, although sallow and morose-looking, was evidently of pacific intent. He paused on the threshold in a kind of surly embarrassment.

"I reckon this is Colonel Starbottle," he said at last, glancing gloomily round him, as if the interview was not entirely of his own seeking. "Well, I've seen you often enough, though you don't know me. My name's Jo Corbin. I guess," he added, still discontentedly, "I have to consult you about something."

"Corbin?" repeated the Colonel in his jauntiest manner. "Ah! Any relation to old Maje Corbin of Nashville, sir?"

"No," said the stranger briefly. "I'm from Shelbyville."

"The Major," continued the Colonel, half closing his eyes as if to follow the Major into the dreamy past, "the old Major, sir, a matter of five or six years ago, was one of my most intimate political friends,—in fact, sir, my most intimate friend. Take a chyar!"

But the stranger had already taken one, and during the Colonel's reminiscence had leaned forward, with his eyes on the ground, discontentedly swinging his soft hat between his legs. "Did you know Tom Frisbee, of Yolo?" he asked abruptly.

"Er—no."

"Nor even heard anything about Frisbee, nor what happened to him?" continued the man, with aggrieved melancholy.

In point of fact the Colonel did not think that he had.

"Nor anything about his being killed over at Fresno?" said the stranger, with a desponding implication that the interview after all was a failure.

"If—er—if you could—er—give me a hint or two,"

suggested the Colonel blandly.

"There wasn't much," said the stranger, "if you don't remember." He paused, then rising, he gloomily dragged his chair slowly beside the table, and taking up a paperweight examined it with heavy dissatisfaction. "You see," he went on slowly, "I killed him—it was a quo'll. He was my pardner, but I reckon he must have drove me hard. Yes, sir," he added with aggrieved reflection, "I reckon he drove me hard."

The Colonel smiled courteously, slightly expanding his chest under the homicidal relation, as if, having taken it in and made it a part of himself, he was ready, if necessary, to become personally responsible for it. Then lifting his empty glass to the light, he looked at it with half closed eyes, in polite imitation of his companion's examination of the paper-weight, and set it down again. A casual spectator from the window might have imagined that the two were engaged in an amicable inventory of the furniture.

"And the—er—actual circumstances?" asked the Colonel.

"Oh, it was fair enough fight. THEY'LL tell you that. And so would HE, I reckon—if he could. He was ugly and bedev'lin', but I didn't care to quo'll, and give him the go-by all the time. He kept on, followed me out of the shanty, drew, and fired twice. I"—he stopped and regarded his hat a moment as if it was a corroborating witness—"I—I closed with him—I had to—it was my only chance, and that ended it—and with his own revolver. I never drew mine."

"I see," said the Colonel, nodding, "clearly justifiable and honorable as regards the code. And you wish me to defend you?"

The stranger's gloomy expression of astonishment now

turned to blank hopelessness.

"I knew you didn't understand," he said, despairingly. "Why, all THAT was TWO YEARS AGO. It's all settled and done and gone. The jury found for me at the inquest. It ain't THAT I want to see you about. It's something arising out of it."

"Ah," said the Colonel, affably, "a vendetta, perhaps. Some friend or relation of his taken up the quarrel?"

The stranger looked abstractedly at Starbottle. "You think a relation might; or would feel in that sort of way?"

"Why, blank it all, sir," said the Colonel, "nothing is more common. Why, in '52 one of my oldest friends, Doctor Byrne, of St. Jo, the seventh in a line from old General Byrne, of St. Louis, was killed, sir, by Pinkey Riggs, seventh in a line from Senator Riggs, of Kentucky. Original cause, sir, something about a d—d roasting ear, or a blank persimmon in 1832; forty-seven men wiped out in twenty years. Fact, sir."

"It ain't that," said the stranger, moving hesitatingly in his chair. "If it was anything of that sort I wouldn't mind,—it might bring matters to a wind-up, and I shouldn't have to come here and have this cursed talk with you."

It was so evident that this frank and unaffected expression of some obscure disgust with his own present position had no other implication, that the Colonel did not except to it. Yet the man did not go on. He stopped and seemed lost in sombre contemplation of his hat.

The Colonel leaned back in his chair, fanned himself elegantly, wiped his forehead with a large pongee hand-kerchief, and looking at his companion, whose shadowed abstraction seemed to render him impervious to the heat, said:—

"My dear Mr. Corbin, I perfectly understand you. Blank it all, sir, the temperature in this infernal hole is quite enough to render any confidential conversation between gentlemen upon delicate matters utterly impossible. It's almost as near Hades, sir, as they make it,—as I trust you and I, Mr. Corbin, will ever experience. I propose," continued the Colonel, with airy geniality, "some light change and refreshment. The bar-keeper of the Magnolia is—er—I may say, sir, facile princeps in the concoction of mint juleps, and there is a back room where I have occasionally conferred with political leaders at election time. It is but a step, sir—in fact, on Main Street—round the corner."

The stranger looked up and then rose mechanically as the Colonel resumed his coat and waistcoat, but not his collar and cravat, which lay limp and dejected among his papers. Then, sheltering himself beneath a large-brimmed Panama hat, and hooking his cane on his arm, he led the way, fan in hand, into the road, tiptoeing in his tight, polished boots through the red, impalpable dust with his usual jaunty manner, yet not without a profane suggestion of burning ploughshares. The stranger strode in silence by his side in the burning sun, impenetrable in his own morose shadow.

But the Magnolia was fragrant, like its namesake, with mint and herbal odors, cool with sprinkled floors, and sparkling with broken ice on its counters, like dewdrops on white, unfolded petals—and slightly soporific with the subdued murmur of droning loungers, who were heavy with its sweets. The gallant Colonel nodded with confidential affability to the spotless-shirted bar-keeper, and then taking Corbin by the arm fraternally conducted him into a small apartment in the rear of the bar-room. It was evidently used as the office of the proprietor, and contained a plain desk, table, and chairs. At the rear window, Nature, not entirely evicted, looked in with a few straggling buckeyes and a dusty myrtle, over the body of a lately-felled pine-tree, that flaunted from an upflung branch a still green spray as if it were a drooping banner lifted by a dead but rigid arm. From the adjoining room the faint, monotonous click of billiard balls, languidly played, came at intervals like the dry notes of cicale in the bushes.

The bar-keeper brought two glasses crowned with mint and diademed with broken ice. The Colonel took a long pull at his portion, and leaned back in his chair with a bland gulp of satisfaction and dreamily patient eyes. The stranger mechanically sipped the contents of his glass, and then, without having altered his reluctant expression, drew from his breast-pocket a number of old letters. Holding them displayed in his fingers like a difficult hand of cards, and with something of the air of a dispirited player, he began:—

"You see, about six months after this yer trouble I got this letter." He picked out a well worn, badly written missive, and put it into Colonel Starbottle's hands, rising at the same time and leaning over him as he read. "You see, she that writ it says as how she hadn't heard from her son for a long time, but owing to his having spoken once about ME, she was emboldened to write and ask me if I knew what had gone of him." He was pointing his finger at each line of the letter as he read it, or rather seemed to translate it from memory with a sad familiarity. "Now," he continued in parenthesis, "you see this kind o' got me. I knew he had got relatives in Kentucky. I knew that all this trouble had been put in the paper with his name and mine, but this here name of Martha Jeffcourt at the bottom didn't seem to jibe with it. Then I remembered that he had left a lot of letters in his trunk in the shanty, and I looked 'em over. And I found that his name

WAS Tom Jeffcourt, and that he'd been passin' under the name of Frisbee all this time."

"Perfectly natural and a frequent occurrence," interposed the Colonel cheerfully. "Only last year I met an old friend whom we'll call Stidger, of New Orleans, at the Union Club, 'Frisco. 'How are you, Stidger?' I said; 'I haven't seen you since we used to meet—driving over the Shell Road in '53.' 'Excuse me, sir,' said he, 'my name is not Stidger, it's Brown.' I looked him in the eye, sir, and saw him quiver. 'Then I must apologize to Stidger,' I said, 'for supposing him capable of changing his name.' He came to me an hour after, all in a tremble. 'For God's sake, Star,' he said,—always called me Star,—'don't go back on me, but you know family affairs—another woman, beautiful creature,' etc., etc.,—yes, sir, perfectly common, but a blank mistake. When a man once funks his own name he'll turn tail on anything. Sorry for this man, Friezecoat, or Turncoat, or whatever's his d—d name; but it's so."

The suggestion did not, however, seem to raise the stranger's spirits or alter his manner. "His name was Jeffcourt, and this here was his mother," he went on drearily; "and you see here she says"—pointing to the letter again—"she's been expecting money from him and it don't come, and she's mighty hard up. And that gave me an idea. I don't know," he went on, regarding the Colonel with gloomy doubt, "as you'll think it was much; I don't know as you wouldn't call it a d—d fool idea, but I got it all the same." He stopped, hesitated, and went on. "You see this man, Frisbee or Jeffcourt, was my pardner. We were good friends up to the killing, and then he drove me hard. I think I told you he drove me hard,—didn't I? Well, he did. But the idea I got was this. Considerin' I killed him after all, and so to speak disappointed them, I reckoned I'd take upon myself the care of that family and send 'em money every month."

The Colonel slightly straitened his clean-shaven mouth. "A kind of expiation or amercement by fine, known to the Mosaic, Roman, and old English law. Gad, sir, the Jews might have made you MARRY his widow or sister. An old custom, and I think superseded—sir, properly superseded—by the alternative of ordeal by battle in the mediaeval times. I don't myself fancy these pecuniary fashions of settling wrongs,—but go on."

"I wrote her," continued Corbin, "that her son was dead, but that he and me had some interests together in a claim, and that I was very glad to know where to send her what would be his share every month. I thought it no use to tell her I killed him,—may be she might refuse to take it. I sent her a hundred dollars every month since. Sometimes it's been pretty hard sleddin' to do it, for I ain't rich; sometimes I've had to borrow the money, but I reckoned that I was only paying for my share in this here business of his bein' dead, and I did it."

"And I understand you that this Jeffcourt really had no interest in your claim?"

Corbin looked at him in dull astonishment. "Not a cent, of course; I thought I told you that. But that weren't his fault, for he never had anything, and owed me money. In fact," he added gloomily, "it was because I hadn't any more to give him—havin' sold my watch for grub—that he quo'lled with me that day, and up and called me a 'sneakin' Yankee hound.' I told you he drove me hard."

The Colonel coughed slightly and resumed his jaunty manner. "And the—er—mother was, of course, grateful and satisfied?"

"Well, no,—not exactly." He stopped again and took up his

letters once more, sorted and arranged them as if to play out his unfinished but hopeless hand, and drawing out another, laid it before the Colonel. "You see, this Mrs. Jeffcourt, after a time, reckoned she ought to have MORE money than I sent her, and wrote saying that she had always understood from her son (he that never wrote but once a year, remember) that this claim of ours (that she never knew of, you know) was paying much more than I sent her—and she wanted a return of accounts and papers, or she'd write to some lawyer, mighty quick. Well, I reckoned that all this was naturally in the line of my trouble, and I DID manage to scrape together fifty dollars more for two months and sent it. But that didn't seem to satisfy her—as you see." He dealt Colonel Starbottle another letter from his baleful hand with an unchanged face. "When I got that,—well, I just up and told her the whole thing. I sent her the account of the fight from the newspapers, and told her as how her son was the Frisbee that was my pardner, and how he never had a cent in the world—but how I'd got that idea to help her, and was willing to carry it out as long as I could."

"Did you keep a copy of that letter?" asked the Colonel, straitening his mask-like mouth.

"No," said Corbin moodily. "What was the good? I know'd she'd got the letter,—and she did,—for that is what she wrote back." He laid another letter before the Colonel, who hastily read a few lines and then brought his fat white hand violently on the desk.

"Why, d—n it all, sir, this is BLACKMAIL! As infamous a case of threatening and chantage as I ever heard of."

"Well," said Corbin, dejectedly, "I don't know. You see she allows that I murdered Frisbee to get hold of his claim, and that I'm trying to buy her off, and that if I don't come down with twenty thousand dollars on the nail, and notes for the rest, she'll prosecute me. Well, mebbe the thing looks to her like that—mebbe you know I've got to shoulder that too. Perhaps it's all in the same line."

Colonel Starbottle for a moment regarded Corbin critically. In spite of his chivalrous attitude towards the homicidal faculty, the Colonel was not optimistic in regard to the baser pecuniary interests of his fellow-man. It was quite on the cards that his companion might have murdered his partner to get possession of the claim. It was true that Corbin had voluntarily assumed an unrecorded and hitherto unknown responsibility that had never been even suspected, and was virtually self-imposed. But that might have been the usual one unerring blunder of criminal sagacity and forethought. It was equally true that he did not look or act like a mean murderer; but that was nothing. However, there was no evidence of these reflections in the Colonel's face. Rather he suddenly beamed with an excess of politeness. "Would you—er—mind, Mr. Corbin, whilst I am going over those letters again, to—er—step across to my office—and—er—bring me the copy of 'Wood's Digest' that lies on my table? It will save some time."

The stranger rose, as if the service was part of his self-imposed trouble, and as equally hopeless with the rest, and taking his hat departed to execute the commission. As soon as he had left the building Colonel Starbottle opened the door and mysteriously beckoned the bar-keeper within.

"Do you remember anything of the killing of a man named Frisbee over in Fresno three years ago?"

The bar-keeper whistled meditatively. "Three years ago—Frisbee?—Fresno?—no? Yes—but that was only one of his names. He was Jack Walker over here. Yes—and by Jove!

that feller that was here with you killed him. Darn my skin, but I thought I recognized him."

"Yes, yes, I know all that," said the Colonel, impatiently. "But did Frisbee have any PROPERTY? Did he have any means of his own?"

"Property?" echoed the bar-keeper with scornful incredulity. "Property? Means? The only property and means he ever had was the free lunches or drinks he took in at somebody else's expense. Why, the only chance he ever had of earning a square meal was when that fellow that was with you just now took him up and made him his partner. And the only way HE could get rid of him was to kill him! And I didn't think he had it in him. Rather a queer kind o' chap,—good deal of hayseed about him. Showed up at the inquest so glum and orkerd that if the boys hadn't made up their minds this yer Frisbee ORTER BEEN killed—it might have gone hard with him."

"Mr. Corbin," said Colonel Starbottle, with a pained but unmistakable hauteur and a singular elevation of his shirt frill, as if it had become of its own accord erectile, "Mr. Corbin—er—er—is the distant relative of old Major Corbin, of Nashville—er—one of my oldest political friends. When Mr. Corbin—er—returns, you can conduct him to me. And, if you please, replenish the glasses."

When the bar-keeper respectfully showed Mr. Corbin and "Wood's Digest" into the room again, the Colonel was still beaming and apologetic.

"A thousand thanks, sir, but except to SHOW you the law if you require it—hardly necessary. I have—er—glanced over the woman's letters again; it would be better, perhaps, if you had kept copies of your own—but still these tell the whole story and YOUR OWN. The claim is preposterous! You have simply to drop the whole thing. Stop your remittances, stop your correspondence,—pay no heed to any further letters and wait results. You need fear nothing further, sir; I stake my professional reputation on it."

The gloom of the stranger seemed only to increase as the Colonel reached his triumphant conclusion.

"I reckoned you'd say that," he said slowly, "but it won't do. I shall go on paying as far as I can. It's my trouble and I'll see it through."

"But, my dear sir, consider," gasped the Colonel. "You are in the hands of an infamous harpy, who is using her son's blood to extract money from you. You have already paid a dozen times more than the life of that d—d sneak was worth; and more than that—the longer you keep on paying you are helping to give color to their claim and estopping your own defense. And Gad, sir, you're making a precedent for this sort of thing! you are offering a premium to widows and orphans. A gentleman won't be able to exchange shots with another without making himself liable for damages. I am willing to admit that your feelings—though, in my opinion—er—exaggerated—do you credit; but I am satisfied that they are utterly misunderstood—sir."

"Not by all of them," said Corbin darkly.

"Eh?" returned the Colonel quickly.

"There was another letter here which I didn't particularly point out to you," said Corbin, taking up the letters again, "for I reckoned it wasn't evidence, so to speak, being from HIS COUSIN, a girl,—and calculated you'd read it when I was out."

The Colonel coughed hastily. "I was in fact—er—just about to glance over it when you came in."

"It was written," continued Corbin, selecting a letter more bethumbed than the others, "after the old woman had threatened me. This here young woman allows that she is sorry that her aunt has to take money of me on account of her cousin being killed, and she is still sorrier that she is so bitter against me. She says she hadn't seen her cousin since he was a boy, and used to play with her, and that she finds it hard to believe that he should ever grow up to change his name and act so as to provoke anybody to lift a hand against him. She says she supposed it must be something in that dreadful California that alters people and makes everybody so reckless. I reckon her head's level there, ain't it?"

There was such a sudden and unexpected lightening of the man's face as he said it, such a momentary relief to his persistent gloom, that the Colonel, albeit inwardly dissenting from both letter and comment, smiled condescendingly.

"She's no slouch of a scribe neither," continued Corbin animatedly. "Read that."

He handed his companion the letter, pointing to a passage with his finger. The Colonel took it with, I fear, a somewhat lowered opinion of his client, and a new theory of the case. It was evident that this weak submission to the aunt's conspiracy was only the result of a greater weakness for the niece. Colonel Starbottle had a wholesome distrust of the sex as a business or political factor. He began to look over the letter, but was evidently slurring it with superficial politeness, when Corbin said:—

"Read it out loud."

The Colonel slightly lifted his shoulders, fortified himself with another sip of the julep, and, leaning back, oratorically began to read,—the stranger leaning over him and following line by line with shining eyes.

"'When I say I am sorry for you, it is because I think it must be dreadful for you to be going round with the blood of a fellow-creature on your hands. It must be awful for you in the stillness of the night season to hear the voice of the Lord saying, "Cain, where is thy brother?" and you saying, "Lord, I have slayed him dead." It must be awful for you when the pride of your wrath was surfitted, and his dum senseless corps was before you, not to know that it is written, "Vengeance is mine, I will repay," saith the Lord. . . . It was no use for you to say, "I never heard that before," remembering your teacher and parents. Yet verily I say unto you, "Though your sins be as scarlet, they shall be washed whiter than snow," saith the Lord—Isaiah i. 18; and "Heart hath no sorrow that Heaven cannot heal."—My hymn book, 1st Presbyterian Church, page 79. Mr. Corbin, I pity your feelins at the grave of my pore dear cousin, knowing he is before his Maker, and you can't bring him back.' Umph!—er—er—very good—very good indeed," said the Colonel, hastily refolding the letter. "Very well meaning and—er"—

"Go on," said Corbin over his shoulder, "you haven't read all."

"Ah, true. I perceive I overlooked something. Um—um. 'May God forgive you, Mr. Corbin, as I do, and make aunty think better of you, for it was good what you tried to do for her and the fammely, and I've always said it when she was raging round and wanting money of you. I don't believe you meant to do it anyway, owin' to your kindness of heart to the ophanless and the widow since you did it. Anser this letter, and don't mind what aunty says. So no more at present from—Yours very respectfully, SALLY DOWS.

"'P. S.—There's been some troubel in our township, and some fitin'. May the Lord change ther hearts and make them as a little child, for if you are still young you may grow up different. I have writ a short prayer for you to say every night. You can coppy it out and put it at the head of your bed. It is this: O Lord make me sorry for having killed Sarah Dows' cousin. Give me, O Lord, that peace that the world cannot give, and which fadeth not away; for my yoke is heavy, and my burden is harder than I can bear.'"

The Colonel's deliberate voice stopped. There was a silence in the room, and the air seemed stifling. The click of the billiard balls came distinctly through the partition from the other room. Then there was another click, a stamp on the floor, and a voice crying coarsely: "Curse it all—missed again!"

To the stranger's astonishment, the Colonel was on his feet in an instant, gasping with inarticulate rage. Flinging the door open, he confronted the startled bar-keeper empurpled and stertorous.

"Blank it all, sir, do you call this a saloon for gentlemen, or a corral for swearing cattle? Or do you mean to say that the conversation of two gentlemen upon delicate professional—and—er—domestic affairs—is to be broken upon by the blank profanity of low-bred hounds over their picayune gambling! Take them my kyard, sir," choked the Colonel, who was always Southern and dialectic in his excited as in his softest moments, "and tell them that Colonel Starbottle will nevah dyarken these doahs again."

Before the astonished bar-keeper could reply, the Colonel had dashed back into the room, clapped his hat on his head, and seized his book, letters, and cane. "Mr. Corbin," he said with gasping dignity, "I will take these papahs, and consult them again in my own office—where, if you will do me the honor, sir, to call at ten o'clock to-morrow, I will give you my opinion." He strode out of the saloon beside the half awe-stricken, half-amused, yet all discreetly silent loungers, followed by his wondering but gloomy client. At the door they parted,—the Colonel tiptoeing towards his office as if dancing with rage, the stranger darkly plodding through the stifling dust in the opposite direction, with what might have been a faint suggestion to his counselor, that the paths of the homicide did not lie beside the still cool waters.

CHAPTER II

The house of Captain Masterton Dows, at Pineville, Kentucky, was a fine specimen of Southern classical architecture, being an exact copy of Major Fauquier's house in Virginia, which was in turn only a slight variation from a well-known statesman's historical villa in Alabama, that everybody knew was designed from a famous Greek temple on the Piraeus. Not but that it shared this resemblance with the County Court House and the Odd Fellows' Hall, but the addition of training jessamine and Cherokee rose to the columns of the portico, and over the colonnade leading to its offices, showed a certain domestic distinction. And the sky line of its incongruously high roof was pleasantly broken against adjacent green pines, butternut, and darker cypress.

A nearer approach showed the stuccoed gateposts—whose red brick core was revealed through the dropping plaster—opening in a wall of half-rough stone, half-wooden palisade, equally covered with shining moss and parasitical vines, which hid a tangled garden left to its own unkempt luxuriance. Yet there was a reminiscence of past formality and even pretentiousness in a wide box-bordered terrace and one or two stuccoed vases prematurely worn and time-stained; while several rare exotics had, however, thriven so unwisely and well in that stimulating soil as to lose their exclusive refinement and acquire a certain temporary vulgarity. A few, with the not uncommon enthusiasm of aliens, had adopted certain native peculiarities with a zeal that far exceeded any indigenous performance. But dominant through all was the continual suggestion of precocious fruition and premature decay that lingered like a sad perfume in the garden, but made itself persistent if less poetical in the house.

Here the fluted wooden columns of the portico and colonnade seemed to have taken upon themselves a sodden and unwholesome age unknown to stone and mortar. Moss and creeper clung to paint that time had neither dried nor mellowed, but left still glairy in its white consistency. There were rusty red blotches around inflamed nail-holes in the swollen wood, as of punctures in living flesh; along the entablature and cornices and in the dank gutters decay had taken the form of a mild deliquescence; and the pillars were spotted as if Nature had dropped over the too early ruin a few unclean tears. The house itself was lifted upon a broad wooden foundation painted to imitate marble with such hopeless mendacity that the architect at the last moment had added a green border, and the owner permitted a fallen board to remain off so as to allow a few privileged fowls to openly explore the interior. When Miss Sally Dows played the piano in the drawing-room she was at times accompanied by the uplifted voice of the sympathetic hounds who sought its quiet retreat in ill-health or low spirits, and from whom she was separated only by an imperfectly carpeted floor of yawning seams. The infant progeny of "Mammy Judy," an old nurse, made this a hiding-place from domestic justice, where they were eventually betrayed by subterranean giggling that had once or twice brought bashful confusion to the hearts of Miss Sally's admirers, and mischievous security to that finished coquette herself.

It was a pleasant September afternoon, on possibly one of these occasions, that Miss Sally, sitting before the piano, alternately striking a few notes with three pink fingers and glancing at her reflection in the polished rosewood surface of the lifted keyboard case, was heard to utter this languid protest:—

"Quit that kind of talk, Chet, unless you just admire to have every word of it repeated all over the county. Those little niggers of Mammy Judy's are lying round somewhere and are mighty 'cute, and sassy, I tell you. It's nothin' to ME, sure, but Miss Hilda mightn't like to hear of it. So soon after your particular attention to her at last night's pawty too."

Here a fresh-looking young fellow of six-and-twenty, leaning uneasily over the piano from the opposite side, was heard to murmur that he didn't care what Miss Hilda heard, nor the whole world, for the matter of that. "But," he added, with a faint smile, "folks allow that you know how to PLAY UP sometimes, and put on the loud pedal, when you don't want Mammy's niggers to hear."

"Indeed," said the young lady demurely. "Like this?"

She put out a distracting little foot, clothed in the white stocking and cool black prunella slipper then de rigueur in the State, and, pressing it on the pedal, began to drum vigorously on the keys. In vain the amorous Chet protested in a voice which the instrument drowned. Perceiving which the artful young lady opened her blue eyes mildly and said:—

"I reckon it IS so; it DOES kind of prevent you hearing what you don't want to hear."

"You know well enough what I mean," said the youth gloomily. "And that ain't all that folks say. They allow that you're doin' a heap too much correspondence with that Californian rough that killed Tom Jeffcourt over there."

"Do they?" said the young lady, with a slight curl of her pretty lip. "Then perhaps they allow that if it wasn't for me he wouldn't be sending a hundred dollars a month to Aunt Martha?"

"Yes," said the fatuous youth; "but they allow he killed Tom for his money. And they do say it's mighty queer doin's in yo' writin' religious letters to him, and Tom your own cousin."

"Oh, they tell those lies HERE, do they? But do they say anything about how, when the same lies were told over in California, the lawyer they've got over there, called Colonel Starbottle,—a Southern man too,—got up and just wrote to Aunt Martha that she'd better quit that afore she got prosecuted? They didn't tell you that, did they, Mister Chester Brooks?"

But here the unfortunate Brooks, after the fashion of all jealous lovers, deserted his allies for his fair enemy. "I don't cotton to what THEY say, Sally, but you DO write to him, and I don't see what you've got to write about—you and him. Jule Jeffcourt says that when you got religion at Louisville during the revival, you felt you had a call to write and save sinners, and you did that as your trial and probation, but that since you backslided and are worldly again, and go to parties, you just keep it up for foolin' and flirtin'! SHE ain't goin' to weaken on the man that shot her brother, just because he's got a gold mine and—a mustache!"

"She takes his MONEY all the same," said Miss Sally.

"SHE don't,—her mother does. SHE says if she was a man she'd have blood for blood!"

"My!" said Miss Sally, in affected consternation. "It's a wonder she don't apply to you to act for her."

"If it was MY brother he killed, I'd challenge him quick enough," said Chet, flushing through his thin pink skin and light hair.

"Marry her, then, and that'll make you one of the family. I reckon Miss Hilda can bear it," rejoined the young lady pertly.

"Look here, Miss Sally," said the young fellow with a boyish despair that was not without a certain pathos in its implied inferiority, "I ain't gifted like you—I ain't on yo' level no how; I can't pass yo' on the road, and so I reckon I must take yo' dust as yo' make it. But there is one thing, Miss Sally, I want to tell you. You know what's going on in this country, you've heard your father say what the opinion of the best men is, and what's likely to happen if the Yanks force that nigger worshiper, Lincoln, on the South. You know that we're drawing the line closer every day, and spottin' the men that ain't sound. Take care, Miss Sally, you ain't sellin' us cheap to some Northern Abolitionist who'd like to set Marm Judy's little niggers to something worse than eavesdropping down there, and mebbe teach 'em to kindle a fire underneath yo' own flo'."

He had become quite dialectic in his appeal, as if youthfully reverting to some accent of the nursery, or as if he were exhorting her in some recognized shibboleth of a section. Miss Sally rose and shut down the piano. Then leaning over it on her elbows, her rounded little chin slightly elevated with languid impertinence, and one saucy foot kicked backwards beyond the hem of her white cotton frock, she said: "And let me tell you, Mister Chester Brooks, that it's just such God-forsaken, infant phenomenons as you who want to run the whole country that make all this fuss, when you ain't no more fit to be trusted with matches than Judy's children. What do YOU know of Mr. Jo Corbin, when you don't even know that he's from Shelbyville, and as good a Suth'ner as you, and if he hasn't got niggers it's because they don't use them in his parts? Yo'r for all the world like one o' Mrs. Johnson's fancy bantams that ain't quit of the shell afore they square off at their own mother. My goodness! Sho! Sho-o-o!" And suiting the action to the word the young lady, still indolently, even in her simulation, swirled around, caught her skirts at the side with each hand, and lazily shaking them before her in the accepted feminine method of frightening chickens as she retreated backwards, dropped them suddenly in a profound curtsey and swept out of the parlor.

Nevertheless, as she entered the sitting-room she paused to listen, then, going to the window, peeped through the slits of the Venetian blind and saw her youthful admirer, more dejected in the consciousness of his wasted efforts and useless attire, mount his showy young horse, as aimlessly spirited as himself, and ride away. Miss Sally did not regret this; neither had she been entirely sincere in her defense of her mysterious correspondent. But, like many of her sex, she was trying to keep up by the active stimulus of opposition an interest that she had begun to think if left to itself might wane. She was conscious that her cousin Julia, although impertinent and illogical, was right in considering her first epistolary advances to Corbin as a youthful convert's religious zeal. But now that her girlish enthusiasm was spent, and the revival itself had proved as fleeting an excitement as the old "Tournament of Love and Beauty," which it had supplanted, she preferred to believe that she enjoyed the fascinating impropriety because it was the actual result of her religious freedom. Perhaps she had a vague idea that Corbin's conversion would expiate her present preference for dress and dancing. She had certainly never flirted with him; they had never exchanged photographs; there was not a passage in his letters that might not have been perused by her parents,—which, I fear, was probably one reason why she had never shown her correspondence; and beyond the fact that this letter-writing gave her a certain importance in her own eyes and those of her companions, it might really be stopped. She even thought of writing at once to him that her parents objected to its further continuance, but remembering that his usual monthly letter was now nearly due, she concluded to wait until it came.

It is to be feared that Miss Sally had little help in the way of family advice, and that the moral administration of the Dows household was as prematurely developed and as precociously exhausted as the estate and mansion themselves. Captain Dows' marriage with Josephine Jeffcourt, the daughter of a "poor white," had been considered a mesalliance by his family, and his own sister, Miranda Dows, had abandoned her brother's roof and refused to associate with the Jeffcourts, only returning to the house and an armed neutrality at the death of Mrs. Dows a few years later. She had taken charge of Miss Sally, sending her to school at Nashville until she was recalled by her father two years ago. It may be imagined that Miss Sally's correspondence with Jeffcourt's murderer had afforded her a mixed satisfaction; it was at first asserted that Miss Sally's forgiveness was really prompted by "Miss Mirandy," as a subtle sarcasm upon the family. When, however, that forgiveness seemed to become a source of revenue to the impoverished Jeffcourts, her Christian interference had declined.

For this reason, possibly, the young girl did not seek her aunt in the bedroom, the dining-room, or the business-room, where Miss Miranda frequently assisted Captain Dows in the fatuous and prejudiced mismanagement of the house and property, nor in any of the vacant guest-rooms, which, in their early wreck of latter-day mahogany and rosewood, seemed to have been unoccupied for ages, but went directly to her own room. This was in the "L," a lately added wing that had escaped the gloomy architectural tyranny of the main building, and gave Miss Sally light, ventilation, the freshness and spice of new pine boards and clean paper, and a separate entrance and windows on a cool veranda all to herself. Intended as a concession to the young lady's traveled taste, it was really a reversion to the finer simplicity of the pioneer.

New as the apartment appeared to be, it was old enough to contain the brief little records of her maidenhood: the childish samplers and pictures; the sporting epoch with its fox-heads, opossum and wild-cat skins, riding-whip, and the goshawk in a cage, which Miss Sally believed could be trained as a falcon; the religious interval of illustrated texts, "Rock of Ages," cardboard crosses, and the certificate of her membership with "The Daughters of Sion" at the head of her little bed, down to the last decadence of frivolity shown in the be-ribboned guitar in the corner, and the dance cards, favors, and rosettes, military buttons, dried bouquets, and other love gages on the mantelpiece.

The young girl opened a drawer of her table and took out a small packet of letters tied up with a green ribbon. As she did so she heard the sound of hoofs in the rear courtyard. This was presently followed by a step on the veranda, and she opened the door to her father with the letters still in her hand. There was neither the least embarrassment nor self-consciousness in her manner.

Captain Dows, superficially remarkable only for a certain odd combination of high military stock and turned-over planter's collar, was slightly exalted by a sympathetic mingling of politics and mint julep at Pineville Court House. "I was passing by the post-office at the Cross Roads last week, dear," he began, cheerfully, "and I thought of you, and reckoned it was about time that my Pussy got one of her letters from her rich Californian friend—and sure enough there was one. I clean forgot to give it to you then, and only remembered it passing there to-day. I didn't get to see if there was any gold-dust in it," he continued, with great archness, and a fatherly pinch of her cheek; "though I suspect that isn't the kind of currency he sends to you."

"It IS from Mr. Corbin," said Miss Sally, taking it with a languid kind of doubt; "and only now, paw, I was just thinking that I'd sort of drop writing any more; it makes a good deal of buzzing amongst the neighbors, and I don't see much honey nor comb in it."

"Eh," said the Captain, apparently more astonished than delighted at his daughter's prudence. "Well, child, suit yourself! It's mighty mean, though, for I was just thinking of telling you that Judge Read is an old friend of this Colonel Starbottle, who is your friend's friend and lawyer, and he says that Colonel Starbottle is WITH US, and working for the cause out there, and has got a list of all the So'thern men in California that are sound and solid for the South. Read says he shouldn't wonder if he'd make California wheel into line too."

"I don't see what that's got to do with Mr. Corbin," said the young girl, impatiently, flicking the still unopened letter against the packet in her hand.

"Well," said the Captain, with cheerful vagueness, "I thought it might interest you,—that's all," and lounged judicially away.

"Paw thinks," said Miss Sally, still standing in the doorway, ostentatiously addressing her pet goshawk, but with one eye following her retreating parent, "Paw thinks that everybody is as keen bent on politics as he is. There's where paw slips up, Jim."

Re-entering the room, scratching her little nose thoughtfully with the edge of Mr. Corbin's letter, she went to the mantel-piece and picked up a small ivory-handled dagger, the gift of Joyce Masterton, aged eighteen, presented with certain verses addressed to a "Daughter of the South," and cut open the envelope. The first glance was at her own name, and then at the signature. There was no change in the formality; it was "Dear Miss Sarah," and "Yours respectfully, Jo Corbin," as usual. She was still secure. But her pretty brows contracted slightly as she read as follows:—

"I've always allowed I should feel easier in my mind if I could ever get to see Mrs. Jeffcourt, and that may be she might feel easier in hers if I stood before her, face to face. Even if she didn't forgive me at once, it might do her good to get off what she had on her mind against me. But as there wasn't any chance of her coming to me, and it was out of the question my coming to her and still keeping up enough work in the mines to send her the regular money, it couldn't be done. But at last I've got a partner to run the machine when I'm away. I shall be at Shelbyville by the time this reaches you, where I shall stay a day or two to give you time to break the news to Mrs. Jeffcourt, and then come on. You will do this for me in your Christian kindness, Miss Dows—won't you? and if you could soften her mind so as to make it less hard for me I shall be grateful.

"P. S.—I forgot to say I have had HIM exhumed—you know who I mean—and am bringing him with me in a patent metallic burial casket,—the best that could be got in 'Frisco, and will see that he is properly buried in your own graveyard. It seemed to me that it would be the best thing I could do, and might work upon her feelings—as it has on mine. Don't you?

"J. C."

Miss Sally felt the tendrils of her fair hair stir with

conster-nation. The letter had arrived a week ago; perhaps he was in Pineville at that very moment! She must go at once to the Jeffcourts,—it was only a mile distant. Perhaps she might be still in time; but even then it was a terribly short notice for such a meeting. Yet she stopped to select her newest hat from the closet, and to tie it with the largest of bows under her pretty chin; and then skipped from the veranda into a green lane that ran beside the garden boundary. There, hidden by a hedge, she dropped into a long, swinging trot, that even in her haste still kept the languid deliberation characteristic of her people, until she had reached the road. Two or three hounds in the garden started joyously to follow her, but she drove them back with a portentous frown, and an ill-aimed stone, and a suppressed voice. Yet in that backward glance she could see that her little Eumenides—Mammy Judy's children—were peering at her from below the wooden floor of the portico, which they were grasping with outstretched arms and bowed shoulders, as if they were black caryatides supporting—as indeed their race had done for many a year—the pre-doomed and decaying mansion of their master.

CHAPTER III

Happily Miss Sally thought more of her present mission than of the past errors of her people. The faster she walked the more vividly she pictured the possible complications of this meeting. She knew the dull, mean nature of her aunt, and the utter hopelessness of all appeal to anything but her selfish cupidity, and saw in this fatuous essay of Corbin only an aggravation of her worst instincts. Even the dead body of her son would not only whet her appetite for pecuniary vengeance, but give it plausibility in the eyes of their emotional but ignorant neighbors. She had still less to hope from Julia Jeffcourt's more honest and human indignation but equally bigoted and prejudiced intelligence. It is true they were only women, and she ought to have no fear of that physical revenge which Julia had spoken of, but she reflected that Miss Jeffcourt's unmistakable beauty, and what was believed to be a "truly Southern spirit," had gained her many admirers who might easily take her wrongs upon their shoulders. If her father had only given her that letter before, she might have stopped Corbin's coming at all; she might even have met him in time to hurry him and her cousin's provocative remains out of the country. In the midst of these reflections she had to pass the little hillside cemetery. It was a spot of great natural beauty, cypress-shadowed and luxuriant. It was justly celebrated in Pineville, and, but for its pretentious tombstones, might have been peaceful and suggestive. Here she recognized a figure just turning from its gate. It was Julia Jeffcourt.

Her first instinct—that she was too late and that her cousin had come to the cemetery to make some arrangements for the impending burial—was, however, quickly dissipated by the young girl's manner.

"Well, Sally Dows, YOU here! who'd have thought of seeing you to-day? Why, Chet Brooks allowed that you danced every set last night and didn't get home till daylight. And you—you that are going to show up at another party to-night too! Well, I reckon I haven't got that much ambition these times. And out with your new bonnet too."

There was a slight curl of her handsome lip as she looked at her cousin. She was certainly a more beautiful girl than Miss Sally; very tall, dark and luminous of eye, with a brunette pallor of complexion, suggesting, it was said, that remote mixture of blood which was one of the unproven counts of Miss Miranda's indictment against her family. Miss Sally smiled sweetly behind her big bow. "If you reckon to tie to everything that Chet Brooks says, you'll want lots of string, and you won't be safe then. You ought to have heard him run on about this one, and that one, and that other one, not an hour ago in our parlor. I had to pack him off, saying he was even making Judy's niggers tired." She stopped and added with polite languor, "I suppose there's no news up at yo' house either? Everything's going on as usual—and—you get yo' California draft regularly?"

A good deal of the white of Julia's beautiful eyes showed as she turned indignantly on the speaker. "I wish, cousin Sally, you'd just let up talking to me about that money. You know as well as I do that I allowed to maw I wouldn't take a cent of it from the first! I might have had all the gowns and bonnets"—with a look at Miss Sally's bows—"I wanted from her; she even offered to take me to St. Louis for a rig-out—if I'd been willing to take blood money. But I'd rather stick to this old sleazy mou'nin' for Tom"—she gave a dramatic pluck at her faded black skirt—"than flaunt round in white muslins and China silks at ten dollars a yard, paid for by his murderer."

"You know black's yo' color always,—taking in your height and complexion, Jule," said Miss Sally demurely, yet not without a feminine consciousness that it really did set off her cousin's graceful figure to perfection. "But you can't keep up this gait always. You know some day you might come upon this Mr. Corbin."

"He'd better not cross my path," she said passionately.

"I've heard girls talk like that about a man and then get just green and yellow after him," said Miss Sally critically. "But goodness me! speaking of meeting people reminds me I clean forgot to stop at the stage office and see about bringing over the new overseer. Lucky I met you, Jule! Good-by, dear. Come in to-night, and we'll all go to the party together." And with a little nod she ran off before her indignant cousin could frame a suitably crushing reply to her Parthian insinuation.

But at the stage office Miss Sally only wrote a few lines on a card, put it in an envelope, which she addressed to Mr. Joseph Corbin, and then seating herself with easy carelessness on a long packing-box, languidly summoned the proprietor.

"You're always on hand yourself at Kirby station when the kyars come in to bring passengers to Pineville, Mr. Sledge?"

"Yes, Miss."

"Yo' haven't brought any strangers over lately?"

"Well, last week Squire Farnham of Green Ridge—if he kin be called a stranger—as used to live in the very house yo father"—

"Yes, I know," said Miss Sally, impatiently, "but if an ENTIRE stranger comes to take a seat for Pineville, you ask him if that's his name," handing the letter, "and give it to him if it is. And—Mr. Sledge—it's nobody's business but—yours and mine."

"I understand, Miss Sally," with a slow, paternal, tolerating wink. "He'll get it, and nobody else, sure."

"Thank you; I hope Mrs. Sledge is getting round again."

"Pow'fully, Miss Sally."

Having thus, as she hoped, stopped the arrival of the unhappy Corbin, Miss Sally returned home to consider the best means of finally disposing of him. She had insisted upon his stopping at Kirby and holding no communication with the Jeffcourts until he heard from her, and had strongly pointed out the hopeless infelicity of his plan. She dare not tell her Aunt Miranda, knowing that she would be too happy to precipitate an interview that would terminate disastrously to both the Jeffcourts and Corbin. She might have to take her father into her confidence,—a dreadful contingency.

She was dressed for the evening party, which was provincially early; indeed, it was scarcely past nine o'clock when she had finished her toilet, when there came a rap at her door. It was one of Mammy Judy's children.
"Dey is a gemplum, Miss Sally."

"Yes, yes," said Miss Sally, impatiently, thinking only of her escort. "I'll be there in a minute. Run away. He can wait."

"And he said I was to guv yo' dis yer," continued the little negro with portentous gravity, presenting a card.

Miss Sally took it with a smile. It was a plain card on which was written with a pencil in a hand she hurriedly recognized, "Joseph Corbin."

Miss Sally's smile became hysterically rigid, and pushing the boy aside with a little cry, she darted along the veranda and entered the parlor from a side door and vestibule. To her momentary relief she saw that her friends had not yet arrived: a single figure—a stranger's—rose as she entered.

Even in her consternation she had time to feel the added shock of disappointment. She had always present in her mind an ideal picture of this man whom she had never seen or even heard described. Joseph Corbin had been tall, dark, with flowing hair and long mustache. He had flashing fiery eyes which were capable of being subdued by a single glance of gentleness—her own. He was tempestuous, quick, and passionate, but in quarrel would be led by a smile. He was a combination of an Italian brigand and a poker player whom she had once met on a Mississippi steamboat. He would wear a broad-brimmed soft hat, a red shirt, showing his massive throat and neck—and high boots! Alas! the man before her was of medium height, with light close-cut hair, hollow cheeks that seemed to have been lately scraped with a razor, and light gray troubled eyes. A suit of cheap black, ill fitting, hastily acquired, and provincial even for Pineville, painfully set off these imperfections, to which a white cravat in a hopelessly tied bow was superadded. A terrible idea that this combination of a country undertaker and an ill-paid circuit preacher on probation was his best holiday tribute to her, and not a funeral offering to Mr. Jeffcourt, took possession of her. And when, with feminine quickness, she saw his eyes wander over her own fine clothes and festal figure, and sink again upon the floor in a kind of hopeless disappointment equal to her own, she felt ready to cry. But the more terrible sound of laughter approaching the house from the garden recalled her. Her friends were coming.

"For Heaven's sake," she broke out desperately, "didn't you get my note at the station telling you not to come?"

His face grew darker, and then took up its look of hopeless resignation, as if this last misfortune was only an accepted part of his greater trouble, as he sat down again, and to Miss Sally's horror, listlessly swung his hat to and fro under his chair.

"No," he said, gloomily, "I didn't go to no station. I walked here all the way from Shelbyville. I thought it might seem more like the square thing to her for me to do. I sent HIM by express ahead in the box. It's been at the stage office all day."

With a sickening conviction that she had been sitting on her cousin's body while she wrote that ill-fated card, the young girl managed to gasp out impatiently: "But you must go—yes—go now, at once! Don't talk now, but go."

"I didn't come here," he said, rising with a kind of slow dignity, "to interfere with things I didn't kalkilate to see," glancing again at her dress, as the voices came nearer, "and that I ain't in touch with,—but to know if you think I'd better bring him—or"—

He did not finish the sentence, for the door had opened suddenly, and a half-dozen laughing girls and their escorts burst into the room. But among them, a little haughty and still irritated from her last interview, was her cousin Julia Jeffcourt, erect and beautiful in a sombre silk.

"Go," repeated Miss Sally, in an agonized whisper. "You must not be known here."

But the attention of Julia had been arrested by her cousin's agitation, and her eye fell on Corbin, where it was fixed with some fatal fascination that seemed in turn to enthrall and possess him also. To Miss Sally's infinite dismay the others fell back and allowed these two black figures to stand out, then to move towards each other with the same terrible magnetism. They were so near she could not repeat her warning to him without the others hearing it. And all hope died when Corbin, turning deliberately towards her with a grave gesture in the direction of Julia, said quietly:—

"Interduce me."

Miss Sally hesitated, and then gasped hastily, "Miss Jeffcourt."

"Yer don't say MY name. Tell her I'm Joseph Corbin of 'Frisco, California, who killed her brother." He stopped and turned towards her. "I came here to try and fix things again—and I've brought HIM."

In the wondering silence that ensued the others smiled vacantly, breathlessly, and expectantly, until Corbin advanced and held out his hand, when Julia Jeffcourt, drawing hers back to her bosom with the palms outward, uttered an inarticulate cry and—and spat in his face!

With that act she found tongue—reviling him, the house that harbored him, the insolence that presented him, the insult that had been put upon her! "Are you men!" she added passionately, "who stand here with the man before you that killed my brother, and see him offer me his filthy villainous hand—and dare not strike him down!"

And they dared not. Violently, blindly, stupidly moved though all their instincts, though they gathered hysterically around him, there was something in his dull self-containment that was unassailable and awful. For he wiped his face and breast with his handkerchief without a tremor, and turned to them with even a suggestion of relief.

"She's right, gentlemen," he said gravely. "She's right. It might have been otherwise. I might have allowed that it might be otherwise,—but she's right. I'm a Soth'n man myself, gentlemen, and I reckon to understand what she has done. I killed the only man that had a right to stand up for her, and she has now to stand up for herself. But if she wants—and you see she allows she wants—to pass that on to some of you, or all of you, I'm willing. As many as you like, and in what way you like—I waive any chyce of weapon—I'm ready, gentlemen. I came here—with HIM—for that purpose."

Perhaps it may have been his fateful resignation; perhaps it may have been his exceeding readiness,—but there was no response. He sat down again, and again swung his hat slowly and gloomily to and fro under his chair.

"I've got him in a box at the stage office," he went on, apparently to the carpet. "I had him dug up that I might bring him here, and mebbe bury some of the trouble and difference along with his friends. It might be," he added, with a slightly glowering upward glance, as to an overruling, but occasionally misdirecting Providence,—"it might be from the way things are piling up on me that some one might have rung in another corpse instead o' HIM, but so far as I can judge, allowin' for the space of time and nat'ral wear and tear—it's HIM!"

He rose slowly and moved towards the door in a silence that was as much the result of some conviction that any violent demonstration against him would be as grotesque and monstrous as the situation, as of anything he had said. Even the flashing indignation of Julia Jeffcourt seemed to become suddenly as unnatural and incongruous as her brother's chief mourner himself, and although she shrank from his passing figure she uttered no word. Chester Brooks's youthful emotions, following the expression of Miss Sally's face, lost themselves in a vague hysteric smile, and the other gentlemen looked sheepish. Joseph Corbin halted at the door.

"Whatever," he said, turning to the company, "ye make up your mind to do about me, I reckon ye'd better do it AFTER the funeral. I'M always ready. But HE, what with being in a box and changing climate, had better go FIRST." He paused, and with a suggestion of delicacy in the momentary dropping of his eyelids, added,—"for REASONS."

He passed out through the door, on to the portico and thence into the garden. It was noticed at the time that the half-dozen hounds lingering there rushed after him with their usual noisy demonstrations, but that they as suddenly stopped, retreated violently to the security of the basement, and there gave relief to their feelings in a succession of prolonged howls.

CHAPTER IV

It must not be supposed that Miss Sally did not feel some contrition over the ineffective part she had played in this last episode. But Joseph Corbin had committed the unpardonable sin to a woman of destroying her own illogical ideas of him, which was worse than if he had affronted the preconceived ideas of others, in which case she might still defend him. Then, too, she was no longer religious, and had no "call" to act as peacemaker. Nevertheless she resented Julia Jeffcourt's insinuations bitterly, and the cousins quarreled—not the first time in their intercourse—and it was reserved for the latter to break the news of Corbin's arrival with the body to Mrs. Jeffcourt.

How this was done and what occurred at that interview has not been recorded. But it was known the next day that, while Mrs. Jeffcourt accepted the body at Corbin's hands,—and it is presumed the funeral expenses also,—he was positively forbidden to appear either at the services at the house or at the church. There had been some wild talk among the younger and many of the lower members of the community, notably the "poor" non-slave-holding whites, of tarring and feathering Joseph Corbin, and riding him on a rail out of the town on the day of the funeral, as a propitiatory sacrifice to the manes of Thomas Jeffcourt; but it being pointed out by the undertaker that it might involve some uncertainty in the settlement of his bill, together with some reasonable doubt of the thorough resignation of Corbin, whose previous momentary aberration in that respect they were celebrating, the project was postponed until AFTER THE FUNERAL. And here an unlooked-for incident occurred.

There was to be a political meeting at Kirby on that day, when certain distinguished Southern leaders had gathered from the remoter Southern States. At the instigation of Captain Dows it was adjourned at the hour of the funeral to enable members to attend, and it was even rumored, to the great delight of Pineville, that a distinguished speaker or two might come over to "improve the occasion" with some slight allusion to the engrossing topic of "Southern Rights." This combined appeal to the domestic and political emotions of Pineville was irresistible. The Second Baptist Church was crowded. After the religious service there was a pause, and Judge Reed, stepping forward amid a breathless silence, said that they were peculiarly honored by the unexpected presence in their midst "of that famous son of the South, Colonel Starbottle," who had lately returned to his native soil from his adopted home in California. Every eye was fixed on the distinguished stranger as he rose.

Jaunty and gallant as ever, femininely smooth-faced, yet polished and high colored as a youthful mask; pectorally expansive, and unfolding the white petals of his waistcoat through the swollen lapels of his coat, like a bursting magnolia bud, Colonel Starbottle began. The present associations were, he might say, singularly hallowed to him; not only was Pineville—a Southern centre—the recognized nursery of Southern chivalry, Southern beauty (a stately inclination to the pew in which Miss Sally and Julia Jeffcourt sat), Southern intelligence, and Southern independence, but it was the home of the lamented dead who had been, like himself and another he should refer to later, an adopted citizen of the Golden State, a seeker of the Golden Fleece, a companion of Jason. It was the home, fellow-citizens and friends, of the sorrowing sister of the deceased, a young lady whom he, the speaker, had as yet known only through the chivalrous blazon of her virtues and graces by her attendant knights (a courteous wave towards the gallery where Joyce Masterton, Chester Brooks, Calhoun Bungstarter, and the embattled youth generally of Pineville became empurpled and idiotic); it was the home of the afflicted widowed mother, also personally unknown to him, but with whom he might say he had had—er—er—professional correspondence. But it was not this alone that hallowed the occasion, it was a sentiment that should speak in trumpet-like tones throughout the South in this uprising of an united section. It was the forgetfulness of petty strife, of family feud, of personal wrongs in the claims of party! It might not be known that he, the speaker, was professionally cognizant of one of these regrettable—should he say accidents?—arising from the chivalrous challenge and equally chivalrous response of two fiery Southern spirits, to which they primarily owe their coming here that day. And he should take it as his duty, his solemn duty, in that sacred edifice to proclaim to the world that in his knowledge as a professional man—as a man of honor, as a Southerner, as a gentleman, that the—er—circumstances which three years ago led to the early demise of our lamented friend and brother, reflected only the highest credit equally on both of the parties. He said this on his own responsibility—in or out of this sacred edifice—and in or out of that sacred edifice he was personally responsible, and prepared to give the fullest satisfaction for it. He was also aware that it might not be known—or understood—that since that boyish episode the survivor had taken the place of the departed in the bereaved family and ministered to their needs with counsel and—er—er—pecuniary aid, and had followed the body afoot across the continent that it might rest with its kindred dust. He was aware that an unchristian—he would say but for that sacred edifice—a DASTARDLY attempt had been made to impugn the survivor's motives—to suggest an unseemly discord between him and the family, but he, the speaker, would never forget the letter breathing with Christian forgiveness and replete with angelic simplicity sent by a member of that family to his client, which came under his professional eye (here the professional eye for a moment lingered on the hysteric face of Miss Sally); he did not envy the head or heart of a man who could peruse these lines—of which the mere recollection—er—er—choked the utterance of even a professional man like—er—himself—without emotion. "And what, my friends and fellow-citizens," suddenly continued the Colonel, replacing his white handkerchief in his coat-tail, "was the reason why my client, Mr. Joseph Corbin—whose delicacy keeps him from appearing among these mourners—comes here to bury all differences, all animosities, all petty passions? Because he is a son of the South; because as a son of the South, as the representative, and a distant connection, I believe, of my old political friend, Major Corbin, of Nashville, he wishes here and everywhere, at this momentous crisis, to sink everything in the one all-pervading, all-absorbing, one and indivisible UNITY of the South in its resistance to the Northern Usurper! That, my friends, is the great, the solemn, the Christian lesson of this most remarkable occasion in my professional, political, and social experience."

Whatever might have been the calmer opinion, there was no doubt that the gallant Colonel had changed the prevailing illogical emotion of Pineville by the substitution of another equally illogical, and Miss Sally was not surprised when her father, touched by the Colonel's allusion to his daughter's epistolary powers, insisted upon bringing Joseph Corbin home with him, and offering him the hospitality of the Dows mansion. Although the stranger seemed to yield rather from the fact that the Dows were relations of the Jeffcourts than from any personal preference, when he was fairly installed in one of the appropriately gloomy guest chambers, Miss Sally set about the delayed work of reconciliation—theoretically accepted by her father, and cynically tolerated by her Aunt Miranda. But here a difficulty arose which she had not foreseen. Although Corbin had evidently forgiven her defection on that memorable evening, he had not apparently got over the revelation of her giddy worldliness, and was resignedly apathetic and distrustful of her endeavors. She was at first amused, and then angry. And her patience was exhausted when she discovered that he actually seemed more anxious to conciliate Julia Jeffcourt than her mother.

"But she spat in your face," she said, indignantly.

"That's so," he replied, gloomily; "but I reckoned you said something in one of your letters about turning the other cheek when you were smitten. Of course, as you don't believe it now," he added with his upward glance, "I suppose THAT'S been played on me, too."

But here Miss Sally's spirit lazily rebelled.

"Look here, Mr. Joseph JEREMIAH Corbin," she returned with languid impertinence, "if instead of cavortin' round on yo' knees trying to conciliate an old woman who never had a stroke of luck till you killed her son, and a young girl who won't be above letting on afore you think it that your conciliatin' her means SPARKIN' her; if instead of that foolishness you'd turn your hand to trying to conciliate the folks here and keep 'em from going into that fool's act of breaking up these United States; if instead of digging up second-hand corpses that's already been put out of sight once you'd set to work to try and prevent the folks about here from digging up their old cranks and their old whims, and their old women fancies, you'd be doing something like a Christian and a man! What's yo' blood-guiltiness—I'd like to know—alongside of the blood-guiltiness of those fools who are just wild to rush into it, led by such turkey-cocks as yo' friend Colonel Starbottle? And you've been five years in California—a free State—and that's all yo' 've toted out of it—a dead body! There now, don't sit there and swing yo' hat under that chyar, but rouse out and come along with me to the pawty if you can shake a foot, and show Miss Pinkney and the gyrls yo' fit for something mo' than to skirmish round as a black japanned spittoon for Julia Jeffcourt!" It is not recorded that Corbin accepted this cheerful invitation, but for a few days afterwards he was more darkly observant of, and respectful to, Miss Sally. Strange indeed if he had not noticed—although always in his resigned fashion—the dull green stagnation of the life around him, or when not accepting it as part of his trouble he had not chafed at the arrested youth and senile childishness of the people. Stranger still if he had not at times been startled to hear the outgrown superstitions and follies of his youth voiced again by grown-up men, and perhaps strangest of all if he had not vaguely accepted it all as the hereditary curse of that barbarism under which he himself had survived and suffered.

The reconciliation between himself and Mrs. Jeffcourt was superficially effected, so far as a daily visit by him to the house indicated it to the community, but it was also known that Julia was invariably absent on these occasions. What happened at those interviews did not transpire, but it may be surmised that Mrs. Jeffcourt, perhaps recognizing the fact that Corbin was really giving her all that he had to give, or possibly having some lurking fear of Colonel Starbottle, was so far placated as to exhibit only the average ingratitude of her species towards a regular benefactor. She consented to the erection of a small obelisk over her son's grave, and permitted Corbin to plant a few flowering shrubs, which he daily visited and took care of. It is said that on one of these pilgrimages he encountered Miss Julia, apparently on the same errand, who haughtily retired. It was further alleged, on the authority of one of Mammy Judy's little niggers, that those two black mourning figures had been seen at nightfall sitting opposite to each other at the head and foot of the grave, and "glowerin'" at one another "like two hants." But when it was asserted on the same authority that their voices had been later overheard uplifted in some vehement discussion over the grave of the impassive dead, great curiosity was aroused. Being pressed by the eager Miss Sally to repeat some words or any words he had heard them say, the little witness glibly replied, "Marse Linkum" (Lincoln), and "The Souf," and so, for the time, shipwrecked his testimony. But it was recalled six months afterwards. It was then that a pleasant spring day brought madness and enthusiasm to a majority of Pineville, and bated breath and awe to a few, and it was known with the tidings that the South had appealed to arms, that among those who had first responded to the call was Joseph Corbin, an alleged "Union man," who had, however, volunteered to take that place in her ranks which might HAVE BEEN FILLED BY THE MAN HE HAD KILLED. And then people forgot all about him.

*****

A year passed. It was the same place; the old familiar outlines of home and garden and landscape. But seen now, in the choking breathlessness of haste, in the fitful changing flashes of life and motion around it, in intervals of sharp suspense or dazed bewilderment, it seemed to be recognized no longer. Men who had known it all their lives, hurrying to the front in compact masses, scurrying to the rear in straggling line, or opening their ranks to let artillery gallop by, stared at it vaguely, and clattered or scrambled on again. The smoke of a masked battery in the woods struggled and writhed to free itself from the clinging treetops behind it, and sank back into a gray encompassing cloud. The dust thrown up by a column of passing horse poured over the wall in one long wave, and whitened the garden with its ashes. Throughout the dim empty house one no longer heard the sound of cannon, only a dull intermittent concussion was felt, silently bringing flakes of plaster from the walls, or sliding fragments of glass from the shattered windows. A shell, lifted from the ominous distance, hung uncertain in the air and then descended swiftly through the roof; the whole house dilated with flame for an instant, smoke rolled slowly from the windows, and even the desolate chimneys started into a hideous mockery of life, and then all was still again. At such awful intervals the sun shone out brightly, touched the green of the still sleeping woods and the red and white of a flower in the garden, and something in a gray uniform writhed out of the dust of the road, staggered to the wall, and died.

A mile down this road, growing more and more obscure with those rising and falling apparitions or the shapeless and rugged heaps terrible in their helpless inertia by hedge and fence, arose the cemetery hill. Taken and retaken thrice that afternoon, the dead above it far outnumbered the dead below; and when at last the tide of battle swept around its base into the dull, reverberating woods, and it emerged from the smoke, silenced and abandoned, only a few stragglers remained. One of them, leaning on his musket, was still gloomily facing the woods.

"Joseph Corbin," said a low, hurried voice.

He started and glanced quickly at the tombs around him. Perhaps it was because he had been thinking of the dead,—but the voice sounded like HIS. Yet it was only the SISTER, who had glided, pale and haggard, from the thicket.

"They are coming through the woods," she said quickly. "Run, or you'll be taken. Why do you linger?"

"You know why," he said gloomily.

"Yes, but you have done yo' duty. You have done his work.

The task is finished now, and yo' free."

He did not reply, but remained gazing at the woods.

"Joseph," she said more gently, laying her trembling hand on his arm, "Joseph, fly—and—take me with you. For I was wrong, and I want you to forgive me. I knew your heart was not in this, and I ought not to have asked you. Joseph—listen! I never wanted to avenge myself nor HIM when I spat on your face. I wanted to avenge myself on HER. I hated her, because I thought she wanted to work upon you and use you for herself."

"Your mother," he said, looking at her.

"No," she said, with widely opened eyes, "you know who I mean—Miss Sally."

He looked at her wonderingly for a moment, but quickly bent his head again in the direction of the road. "They are coming," he said, starting. "YOU must go. This is no place for you. Stop! it's too late; you cannot go now until they have passed. Come here—crouch down here—over this grave—so."

He almost forced her—kneeling down—upon the mound below the level of the shrubs, and then ran quickly himself a few paces lower down the hill to a more exposed position. She understood it. He wished to attract attention to himself. He was successful—a few hurried shots followed from the road, but struck above him.

He clambered back quickly to where she was still crouching.

"They were the vedettes," he said, "but they have fallen back on the main skirmish line and will be here in force in a moment. Go—while you can." She had not moved. He tried to raise her—her hat fell off—he saw blood oozing from where the vedette's bullet that had missed him had pierced her brain.

And yet he saw in that pale dead face only the other face which he remembered now had been turned like this towards his own. It was very strange. And this was the end, and this was his expiation! He raised his own face humbly, blindly, despairingly to the inscrutable sky; it looked back upon him from above as coldly as the dead face had from below.

Yet out of this he struck a faint idea that he voiced aloud in nearly the same words which he had used to Colonel Starbottle only three years ago. "It was with his own pistol too," he said, and took up his musket.

He walked deliberately down the hill, occasionally trying the stock of his musket in the loose earth, and at last suddenly remained motionless, in the attitude of leaning over it. At the same moment there was a distant shout; two thin parallel streams of blue and steel came issuing through the woods like a river, appeared to join tumultuously in the open before the hill, and out of the tumult a mounted officer called upon him to surrender.

He did not reply.

"Come down from there, Johnny Reb, I want to speak to you," called a young corporal.

He did not move.

"It's time to go home, Johnny."

No response.

The officer, who had been holding down his men with an unsworded but masterful hand, raised it suddenly. A dozen shots followed. The men leaped forward, and dashing Corbin contemptuously aside streamed up the hill past him.

But he had neither heard nor cared. For they found he had already deliberately transfixed himself through the heart on his own bayonet.

THE POSTMISTRESS OF LAUREL RUN

CHAPTER I

The mail stage had just passed Laurel Run,—so rapidly that the whirling cloud of dust dragged with it down the steep grade from the summit hung over the level long after the stage had vanished, and then, drifting away, slowly sifted a red precipitate over the hot platform of the Laurel Run post-office.

Out of this cloud presently emerged the neat figure of the postmistress with the mailbag which had been dexterously flung at her feet from the top of the passing vehicle. A dozen loungers eagerly stretched out their hands to assist her, but the warning: "It's agin the rules, boys, for any but her to touch it," from a bystander, and a coquettish shake of the head from the postmistress herself—much more effective than any official interdict—withheld them. The bag was not heavy,—Laurel Run was too recent a settlement to have attracted much correspondence,—and the young woman, having pounced upon her prey with a certain feline instinct, dragged it, not without difficulty, behind the partitioned inclosure in the office, and locked the door. Her pretty face, momentarily visible through the window, was slightly flushed with the exertion, and the loose ends of her fair hair, wet with perspiration, curled themselves over her forehead into tantalizing little rings. But the window shutter was quickly closed, and this momentary but charming vision withdrawn from the waiting public.

"Guv'ment oughter have more sense than to make a woman pick mail-bags outer the road," said Jo Simmons sympathetically. "'Tain't in her day's work anyhow; Guv'mont oughter hand 'em over to her like a lady; it's rich enough and ugly enough."

"'Tain't Guv'ment; it's that stage company's airs and graces," interrupted a newcomer. "They think it mighty fine to go beltin' by, makin' everybody take their dust, just because STOPPIN' ain't in their contract. Why, if that expressman who chucked down the bag had any feelin's for a lady"—but he stopped here at the amused faces of his auditors.

"Guess you don't know much o' that expressman's feelin's, stranger," said Simmons grimly. "Why, you oughter see him just nussin' that bag like a baby as he comes tearin' down the grade, and then rise up and sorter heave it to Mrs. Baker ez if it was a five-dollar bokay! His feelin's for her! Why, he's give himself so dead away to her that we're looking for him to forget what he's doin' next, and just come sailin' down hisself at her feet."

Meanwhile, on the other side of the partition, Mrs. Baker had brushed the red dust from the padlocked bag, and removed what seemed to be a supplementary package attached to it by a wire. Opening it she found a handsome scent-bottle, evidently a superadded gift from the devoted expressman. This she put aside with a slight smile and the murmured word, "Foolishness." But when she had unlocked the bag, even its sacred interior was also profaned by a covert parcel from the adjacent postmaster at Burnt Ridge, containing a gold "specimen" brooch and some circus tickets. It was laid aside with the other. This also was vanity and—presumably—vexation of spirit.

There were seventeen letters in all, of which five were for herself—and yet the proportion was small that morning. Two of them were marked "Official Business" and were promptly put by with feminine discernment; but in another compartment than that holding the presents. Then the shutter was opened, and the task of delivery commenced.

It was accompanied with a social peculiarity that had in time become a habit of Laurel Run. As the young woman delivered the letters, in turn, to the men who were patiently drawn up in Indian file, she made that simple act a medium of privileged but limited conversation on special or general topics,—gay or serious as the case might be, or the temperament of the man suggested. That it was almost always of a complimentary character on their part may be readily imagined; but it was invariably characterized by an element of refined restraint, and, whether from some implied understanding or individual sense of honour, it never passed the bounds of conventionality or a certain delicacy of respect. The delivery was consequently more or less protracted, but when each man had exchanged his three or four minutes' conversation with the fair postmistress,—a conversation at times impeded by bashfulness or timidity, on his part solely, or restricted often to vague smiling,—he resignedly made way for the next. It was a formal levee, mitigated by the informality of rustic tact, great good-humor, and infinite patience, and would have been amusing had it not always been terribly in earnest and at times touching. For it was peculiar to the place and the epoch, and indeed implied the whole history of Mrs. Baker.

She was the wife of John Baker, foreman of "The Last

Chance," now for a year lying dead under half a mile of crushed and beaten-in tunnel at Burnt Ridge. There had been a sudden outcry from the depths at high hot noontide one day, and John had rushed from his cabin—his young, foolish, flirting wife clinging to him—to answer that despairing cry of his imprisoned men. There was one exit that he alone knew which might be yet held open, among falling walls and tottering timbers, long enough to set them free. For one moment only the strong man hesitated between her entreating arms and his brothers' despairing cry. But she rose suddenly with a pale face, and said, "Go, John; I will wait for you here." He went, the men were freed—but she had waited for him ever since!

Yet in the shock of the calamity and in the after struggles of that poverty which had come to the ruined camp, she had scarcely changed. But the men had. Although she was to all appearances the same giddy, pretty Betsy Baker, who had been so disturbing to the younger members, they seemed to be no longer disturbed by her. A certain subdued awe and respect, as if the martyred spirit of John Baker still held his arm around her, appeared to have come upon them all. They held their breath as this pretty woman, whose brief mourning had not seemed to affect her cheerfulness or even playfulness of spirit, passed before them. But she stood by her cabin and the camp—the only woman in a settlement of forty men—during the darkest hours of their fortune. Helping them to wash and cook, and ministering to their domestic needs, the sanctity of her cabin was, however, always kept as inviolable as if it had been HIS tomb. No one exactly knew why, for it was only a tacit instinct; but even one or two who had not scrupled to pay court to Betsy Baker during John Baker's life, shrank from even a suggestion of familiarity towards the woman who had said that she would "wait for him there."

When brighter days came and the settlement had increased

by one or two families, and laggard capital had been hurried up to relieve the still beleaguered and locked-up wealth of Burnt Ridge, the needs of the community and the claims of the widow of John Baker were so well told in political quarters that the post-office of Laurel Run was created expressly for her. Every man participated in the building of the pretty yet substantial edifice—the only public building of Laurel Run—that stood in the dust of the great highway, half a mile from the settlement. There she was installed for certain hours of the day, for she could not be prevailed upon to abandon John's cabin, and here, with all the added respect due to a public functionary, she was secure in her privacy.

But the blind devotion of Laurel Run to John Baker's relict did not stop here. In its zeal to assure the Government authorities of the necessity for a post-office, and to secure a permanent competency to the postmistress, there was much embarrassing extravagance. During the first week the sale of stamps at Laurel Run post-office was unprecedented in the annals of the Department. Fancy prices were given for the first issue; then they were bought wildly, recklessly, unprofitably, and on all occasions. Complimentary congratulation at the little window invariably ended with "and a dollar's worth of stamps, Mrs. Baker." It was felt to be supremely delicate to buy only the highest priced stamps, without reference to their adequacy; then mere QUANTITY was sought; then outgoing letters were all over-paid and stamped in outrageous proportion to their weight and even size. The imbecility of this, and its probable effect on the reputation of Laurel Run at the General Post-office, being pointed out by Mrs. Baker, stamps were adopted as local currency, and even for decorative purposes on mirrors and the walls of cabins. Everybody wrote letters, with the result, however, that those SENT were ludicrously and suspiciously in excess of those received. To obviate this, select parties made forced journeys to Hickory Hill, the next post-office, with letters and circulars addressed to themselves at Laurel Run. How long the extravagance would have continued is not known, but it was not until it was rumored that, in consequence of this excessive flow of business, the Department had concluded that a postMASTER would be better fitted for the place that it abated, and a compromise was effected with the General Office by a permanent salary to the postmistress.

Such was the history of Mrs. Baker, who had just finished her afternoon levee, nodded a smiling "good-by" to her last customer, and closed her shutter again. Then she took up her own letters, but, before reading them, glanced, with a pretty impatience, at the two official envelopes addressed to herself, which she had shelved. They were generally a "lot of new rules," or notifications, or "absurd" questions which had nothing to do with Laurel Run and only bothered her and "made her head ache," and she had usually referred them to her admiring neighbor at Hickory Hill for explanation, who had generally returned them to her with the brief indorsement, "Purp stuff, don't bother," or, "Hog wash, let it slide." She remembered now that he had not returned the last two. With knitted brows and a slight pout she put aside her private correspondence and tore open the first one. It referred with official curtness to an unanswered communication of the previous week, and was "compelled to remind her of rule 47." Again those horrid rules! She opened the other; the frown deepened on her brow, and became fixed.

It was a summary of certain valuable money letters that had miscarried on the route, and of which they had given her previous information. For a moment her cheeks blazed. How dare they; what did they mean! Her waybills and register were always right; she knew the names of every man, woman, and child in her district; no such names as those borne by the missing letters had ever existed at Laurel Run; no such addresses had ever been sent from Laurel Run post-office. It was a mean insinuation! She would send in her resignation at once! She would get "the boys" to write an insulting letter to Senator Slocumb,—Mrs. Baker had the feminine idea of Government as a purely personal institution,—and she would find out who it was that had put them up to this prying, crawling impudence! It was probably that wall-eyed old wife of the postmaster at Heavy Tree Crossing, who was jealous of her. "Remind her of their previous unanswered communication," indeed! Where was that communication, anyway? She remembered she had sent it to her admirer at Hickory Hill. Odd that he hadn't answered it. Of course, he knew about this meanness—could he, too, have dared to suspect her! The thought turned her crimson again. He, Stanton Green, was an old "Laurel Runner," a friend of John's, a little "triflin'" and "presoomin'," but still an old loyal pioneer of the camp! "Why hadn't he spoke up?"

There was the soft, muffled fall of a horse's hoof in the thick dust of the highway, the jingle of dismounting spurs, and a firm tread on the platform. No doubt one of the boys returning for a few supplemental remarks under the feeble pretense of forgotten stamps. It had been done before, and she had resented it as "cayotin' round;" but now she was eager to pour out her wrongs to the first comer. She had her hand impulsively on the door of the partition, when she stopped with a new sense of her impaired dignity. Could she confess this to her worshipers? But here the door opened in her very face, and a stranger entered.

He was a man of fifty, compactly and strongly built. A squarely-cut goatee, slightly streaked with gray, fell straight from his thin-lipped but handsome mouth; his eyes were dark, humorous, yet searching. But the distinctive quality that struck Mrs Baker was the blending of urban ease with frontier frankness. He was evidently a man who had seen cities and knew countries as well. And while he was dressed with the comfortable simplicity of a Californian mounted traveler, her inexperienced but feminine eye detected the keynote of his respectability in the carefully-tied bow of his cravat. The Sierrean throat was apt to be open, free, and unfettered.

"Good-morning, Mrs. Baker," he said, pleasantly, with his hat already in his hand, "I'm Harry Home, of San Francisco." As he spoke his eye swept approvingly over the neat inclosure, the primly-tied papers, and well-kept pigeon-holes; the pot of flowers on her desk; her china-silk mantle, and killing little chip hat and ribbons hanging against the wall; thence to her own pink, flushed face, bright blue eyes, tendriled clinging hair, and then—fell upon the leathern mailbag still lying across the table. Here it became fixed on the unfortunate wire of the amorous expressman that yet remained hanging from the brass wards of the lock, and he reached his hand toward it.

But little Mrs. Baker was before him, and had seized it in her arms. She had been too preoccupied and bewildered to resent his first intrusion behind the partition, but this last familiarity with her sacred official property—albeit empty—capped the climax of her wrongs.

"How dare you touch it!" she said indignantly. "How dare you come in here! Who are you, anyway? Go outside, at once!"

The stranger fell back with an amused, deprecatory gesture, and a long silent laugh. "I'm afraid you don't know me, after all!" he said pleasantly. "I'm Harry Home, the Department Agent from the San Francisco office. My note of advice, No. 201, with my name on the envelope, seems to have miscarried too."

Even in her fright and astonishment it flashed upon Mrs. Baker that she had sent that notice, too, to Hickory Hill. But with it all the feminine secretive instinct within her was now thoroughly aroused, and she kept silent.

"I ought to have explained," he went on smilingly; "but you are quite right, Mrs. Baker," he added, nodding towards the bag. "As far as you knew, I had no business to go near it. Glad to see you know how to defend Uncle Sam's property so well. I was only a bit puzzled to know" (pointing to the wire) "if that thing was on the bag when it was delivered to you?"

Mrs. Baker saw no reason to conceal the truth. After all, this official was a man like the others, and it was just as well that he should understand her power. "It's only the expressman's foolishness," she said, with a slightly coquettish toss of her head. "He thinks it smart to tie some nonsense on that bag with the wire when he flings it down."

Mr. Home, with his eyes on her pretty face, seemed to think it a not inhuman or unpardonable folly. "As long as he doesn't meddle with the inside of the bag, I suppose you must put up with it," he said laughingly. A dreadful recollection, that the Hickory Hill postmaster had used the inside of the bag to convey HIS foolishness, came across her. It would never do to confess it now. Her face must have shown some agitation, for the official resumed with a half-paternal, half-reassuring air: "But enough of this. Now, Mrs. Baker, to come to my business here. Briefly, then, it doesn't concern you in the least, except so far as it may relieve you and some others, whom the Department knows equally well, from a certain responsibility, and, perhaps, anxiety. We are pretty well posted down there in all that concerns Laurel Run, and I think" (with a slight bow) "we've known all about you and John Baker. My only business here is to take your place to-night in receiving the 'Omnibus Way Bag,' that you know arrives here at 9.30, doesn't it?"

"Yes, sir," said Mrs. Baker hurriedly; "but it never has anything for us, except"—(she caught herself up quickly, with a stammer, as she remembered the sighing Green's occasional offerings) "except a notification from Hickory Hill post-office. It leaves there," she went on with an affectation of precision, "at half past eight exactly, and it's about an hour's run—seven miles by road."

"Exactly," said Mr. Home. "Well, I will receive the bag, open it, and dispatch it again. You can, if you choose, take a holiday."

"But," said Mrs. Baker, as she remembered that Laurel Run always made a point of attending her evening levee on account of the superior leisure it offered, "there are the people who come for letters, you know."

"I thought you said there were no letters at that time," said Mr. Home quickly.

"No—but—but"—(with a slight hysterical stammer) "the boys come all the same."

"Oh!" said Mr. Home dryly.

"And—O Lord!"—But here the spectacle of the possible discomfiture of Laurel Run at meeting the bearded face of Mr. Home, instead of her own smooth cheeks, at the window, combined with her nervous excitement, overcame her so that, throwing her little frilled apron over her head, she gave way to a paroxym of hysterical laughter. Mr. Home waited with amused toleration for it to stop, and, when she had recovered, resumed. "Now, I should like to refer an instant to my first communication to you. Have you got it handy?"

Mrs. Baker's face fell. "No; I sent it over to Mr. Green, of Hickory Hill, for information."

"What!"

Terrified at the sudden seriousness of the man's voice, she managed to gasp out, however, that, after her usual habit, she had not opened the official letters, but had sent them to her more experienced colleague for advice and information; that she never could understand them herself,—they made her head ache, and interfered with her other duties,—but HE understood them, and sent her word what to do. Remembering also his usual style of indorsement, she grew red again.

"And what did he say?"

"Nothing; he didn't return them."

"Naturally," said Mr. Home, with a peculiar expression. After a few moments' silent stroking of his beard, he suddenly faced the frightened woman.

"You oblige me, Mrs. Baker, to speak more frankly to you than I had intended. You have—unwittingly, I believe—given information to a man whom the Government suspects of peculation. You have, without knowing it, warned the postmaster at Hickory Hill that he is suspected; and, as you might have frustrated our plans for tracing a series of embezzlements to their proper source, you will see that you might have also done great wrong to yourself as his only neighbor and the next responsible person. In plain words, we have traced the disappearance of money letters to a point when it lies between these two offices. Now, I have not the least hesitation in telling you that we do not suspect Laurel Run, and never have suspected it. Even the result of your thoughtless act, although it warned him, confirms our suspicion of his guilt. As to the warning, it has failed, or he has grown reckless, for another letter has been missed since. To-night, however, will settle all doubt in the matter. When I open that bag in this office to-night, and do not find a certain decoy letter in it, which was last checked at Heavy Tree Crossing, I shall know that it remains in Green's possession at Hickory Hill."

She was sitting back in her chair, white and breathless. He glanced at her kindly, and then took up his hat. "Come, Mrs. Baker, don't let this worry you. As I told you at first, YOU have nothing to fear. Even your thoughtlessness and ignorance of rules have contributed to show your own innocence. Nobody will ever be the wiser for this; we do not advertise our affairs in the Department. Not a soul but yourself knows the real cause of my visit here. I will leave you here alone for a while, so as to divert any suspicion. You will come, as usual, this evening, and be seen by your friends; I will only be here when the bag arrives, to open it. Good-by, Mrs. Baker; it's a nasty bit of business, but it's all in the day's work. I've seen worse, and, thank God, you're out of it."

She heard his footsteps retreat into the outer office and die out of the platform; the jingle of his spurs, and the hollow beat of his horse's hoofs that seemed to find a dull echo in her own heart, and she was alone.

The room was very hot and very quiet; she could hear the warping and creaking of the shingles under the relaxing of the nearly level sunbeams. The office clock struck seven. In the breathless silence that followed, a woodpecker took up his interrupted work on the roof, and seemed to beat out monotonously on her ear the last words of the stranger: Stanton Green—a thief! Stanton Green, one of the "boys" John had helped out of the falling tunnel! Stanton Green, whose old mother in the States still wrote letters to him at Laurel Run, in a few hours to be a disgraced and ruined man forever! She remembered now, as a thoughtless woman remembers, tales of his extravagance and fast living, of which she had taken no heed, and, with a sense of shame, of presents sent her, that she now clearly saw must have been far beyond his means. What would the boys say? What would John have said? Ah! what would John have DONE!

She started suddenly to her feet, white and cold as on that day that she had parted from John Baker before the tunnel. She put on her hat and mantle, and going to that little iron safe that stood in the corner, unlocked it and took out its entire contents of gold and silver. She had reached the door when another idea seized her, and opening her desk she collected her stamps to the last sheet, and hurriedly rolled them up under her cape. Then with a glance at the clock, and a rapid survey of the road from the platform, she slipped from it, and seemed to be swallowed up in the waiting woods beyond.

CHAPTER II

Once within the friendly shadows of the long belt of pines, Mrs. Baker kept them until she had left the limited settlement of Laurel Run far to the right, and came upon an open slope of Burnt Ridge, where she knew Jo Simmons' mustang, Blue Lightning, would be quietly feeding. She had often ridden him before, and when she had detached the fifty-foot reata from his head-stall, he permitted her the further recognized familiarity of twining her fingers in his bluish mane and climbing on his back. The tool-shed of Burnt Ridge Tunnel, where Jo's saddle and bridle always hung, was but a canter farther on. She reached it unperceived, and—another trick of the old days—quickly extemporized a side-saddle from Simmons' Mexican tree, with its high cantle and horn bow, and the aid of a blanket. Then leaping to her seat, she rapidly threw off her mantle, tied it by its sleeves around her waist, tucked it under one knee, and let it fall over her horse's flanks. By this time Blue Lightning was also struck with a flash of equine recollection and pricked up his ears. Mrs. Baker uttered a little chirping cry which he remembered, and the next moment they were both careering over the Ridge.

The trail that she had taken, though precipitate, difficult, and dangerous in places, was a clear gain of two miles on the stage road. There was less chance of her being followed or meeting any one. The greater canyons were already in shadow; the pines on the farther ridges were separating their masses, and showing individual silhouettes against the sky, but the air was still warm, and the cool breath of night, as she well knew it, had not yet begun to flow down the mountain. The lower range of Burnt Ridge was still uneclipsed by the creeping shadow of the mountain ahead of her. Without a watch, but with this familiar and slowly changing dial spread out before her, she knew the time to a minute. Heavy Tree

Hill, a lesser height in the distance, was already wiped out by that shadowy index finger—half past seven! The stage would be at Hickory Hill just before half past eight; she ought to anticipate it, if possible,—it would stay ten minutes to change horses,—she MUST arrive before it left!

There was a good two-mile level before the rise of the next range. Now, Blue Lightning! all you know! And that was much,—for with the little chip hat and fluttering ribbons well bent down over the bluish mane, and the streaming gauze of her mantle almost level with the horse's back, she swept down across the long tableland like a skimming blue-jay. A few more bird-like dips up and down the undulations, and then came the long, cruel ascent of the Divide.

Acrid with perspiration, caking with dust, slithering in the slippery, impalpable powder of the road, groggily staggering in a red dusty dream, coughing, snorting, head-tossing; becoming suddenly dejected, with slouching haunch and limp legs on easy slopes, or wildly spasmodic and agile on sharp acclivities, Blue Lightning began to have ideas and recollections! Ah! she was a devil for a lark—this lightly-clinging, caressing, blarneying, cooing creature—up there! He remembered her now. Ha! very well then. Hoop-la! And suddenly leaping out like a rabbit, bucking, trotting hard, ambling lightly, "loping" on three legs and recreating himself,—as only a California mustang could,—the invincible Blue Lightning at last stood triumphantly upon the summit. The evening star had just pricked itself through the golden mist of the horizon line,—eight o'clock! She could do it now! But here, suddenly, her first hesitation seized her. She knew her horse, she knew the trail, she knew herself,—but did she know THE MAN to whom she was riding? A cold chill crept over her, and then she shivered in a sudden blast; it was Night at last swooping down from the now invisible Sierras, and possessing all it touched. But it was only one long descent to Hickory Hill now, and she swept down securely on its wings. Half-past eight! The lights of the settlement were just ahead of her—but so, too, were the two lamps of the waiting stage before the post-office and hotel.

Happily the lounging crowd were gathered around the hotel, and she slipped into the post-office from the rear, unperceived. As she stepped behind the partition, its only occupant—a good-looking young fellow with a reddish mustache—turned towards her with a flush of delighted surprise. But it changed at the sight of the white, determined face and the brilliant eyes that had never looked once towards him, but were fixed upon a large bag, whose yawning mouth was still open and propped up beside his desk.

"Where is the through money letter that came in that bag?" she said quickly.

"What—do—you—mean?" he stammered, with a face that had suddenly grown whiter than her own.

"I mean that it's a DECOY, checked at Heavy Tree Crossing, and that Mr. Home, of San Francisco, is now waiting at my office to know if you have taken it!"

The laugh and lie that he had at first tried to summon to mouth and lips never reached them. For, under the spell of her rigid, truthful face, he turned almost mechanically to his desk, and took out a package.

"Good God! you've opened it already!" she cried, pointing to the broken seal.

The expression on her face, more than anything she had said, convinced him that she knew all. He stammered under the new alarm that her despairing tone suggested. "Yes!—I was owing some bills—the collector was waiting here for the money, and I took something from the packet. But I was going to make it up by next mail—I swear it."

"How much have you taken?"

"Only a trifle. I"—

"How much?"

"A hundred dollars!"

She dragged the money she had brought from Laurel Run from her pocket, and counting out the sum, replaced it in the open package. He ran quickly to get the sealing wax, but she motioned him away as she dropped the package back into the mail-bag. "No; as long as the money is found in the bag the package may have been broken ACCIDENTALLY. Now burst open one or two of those other packages a little—so;" she took out a packet of letters and bruised their official wrappings under her little foot until the tape fastening was loosened. "Now give me something heavy." She caught up a brass two-pound weight, and in the same feverish but collected haste wrapped it in paper, sealed it, stamped it, and, addressing it in a large printed hand to herself at Laurel Hill, dropped it in the bag. Then she closed it and locked it; he would have assisted her, but she again waved him away. "Send for the expressman, and keep yourself out of the way for a moment," she said curtly.

An attitude of weak admiration and foolish passion had taken the place of his former tremulous fear. He obeyed excitedly, but without a word. Mrs. Baker wiped her moist forehead and parched lips, and shook out her skirt. Well might the young expressman start at the unexpected revelation of those sparkling eyes and that demurely smiling mouth at the little window.

"Mrs. Baker!"

She put her finger quickly to her lips, and threw a world of unutterable and enigmatical meaning into her mischievous face.

"There's a big San Francisco swell takin' my place at Laurel to-night, Charley."

"Yes, ma'am."

"And it's a pity that the Omnibus Way Bag happened to get such a shaking up and banging round already, coming here."

"Eh?"

"I say," continued Mrs. Baker, with great gravity and dancing eyes, "that it would be just AWFUL if that keerful city clerk found things kinder mixed up inside when he comes to open it. I wouldn't give him trouble for the world, Charley."

"No, ma'am, it ain't like you."

"So you'll be particularly careful on MY account."

"Mrs. Baker," said Charley, with infinite gravity, "if that bag SHOULD TUMBLE OFF A DOZEN TIMES between this and Laurel Hill, I'll hop down and pick it up myself."

"Thank you! shake!"

They shook hands gravely across the window-ledge.

"And you ain't going down with us, Mrs. Baker?"

"Of course not; it wouldn't do,—for I AIN'T HERE,—don't you see?"

"Of course!"

She handed him the bag through the door. He took it carefully, but in spite of his great precaution fell over it twice on his way to the road, where from certain exclamations and shouts it seemed that a like miserable mischance attended its elevation to the boot. Then Mrs. Baker came back into the office, and, as the wheels rolled away, threw herself into a chair, and inconsistently gave way for the first time to an outburst of tears. Then her hand was grasped suddenly and she found Green on his knees before her. She started to her feet.

"Don't move," he said, with weak hysteric passion, "but listen to me, for God's sake! I am ruined, I know, even though you have just saved me from detection and disgrace. I have been mad!—a fool, to do what I have done, I know, but you do not know all—you do not know why I did it—you cannot think of the temptation that has driven me to it. Listen, Mrs. Baker. I have been striving to get money, honestly, dishonestly—any way, to look well in YOUR eyes—to make myself worthy of you—to make myself rich, and to be able to offer you a home and take you away from Laurel Run. It was all for YOU, it was all for love of YOU, Betsy, my darling. Listen to me!"

In the fury, outraged sensibility, indignation, and infinite disgust that filled her little body at that moment, she should have been large, imperious, goddess-like, and commanding. But God is at times ironical with suffering womanhood. She could only writhe her hand from his grasp with childish contortions; she could only glare at him with eyes that were prettily and piquantly brilliant; she could only slap at his detaining hand with a plump and velvety palm, and when she found her voice it was high falsetto. And all she could say was, "Leave me be, looney, or I'll scream!"

He rose, with a weak, confused laugh, half of miserable affectation and half of real anger and shame.

"What did you come riding over here for, then? What did you take all this risk for? Why did you rush over here to share my disgrace—for YOU are as much mixed up with this now as I am—if you didn't calculate to share EVERYTHING ELSE with me? What did you come here for, then, if not for ME?"

"What did I come here for?" said Mrs. Baker, with every drop of red blood gone from her cheek and trembling lip. "What—did—I—come here for? Well!—I came here for JOHN BAKER'S sake! John Baker, who stood between you and death at Burnt Ridge, as I stand between you and damnation at Laurel Run, Mr. Green! Yes, John Baker, lying under half of Burnt Ridge, but more to me this day than any living man crawling over it—in—in"—oh, fatal climax!—"in a month o' Sundays! What did I come here for? I came here as John Baker's livin' wife to carry on dead John Baker's work. Yes, dirty work this time, may be, Mr. Green! but his work and for HIM only—precious! That's what I came here for; that's what I LIVE for; that's what I'm waiting for—to be up to HIM and his work always! That's me—Betsy Baker!"

She walked up and down rapidly, tying her chip hat under her chin again. Then she stopped, and taking her chamois purse from her pocket, laid it sharply on the desk.

"Stanton Green, don't be a fool! Rise up out of this, and be a man again. Take enough out o' that bag to pay what you owe Gov'ment, send in your resignation, and keep the rest to start you in an honest life elsewhere. But light out o' Hickory Hill afore this time to-morrow."

She pulled her mantle from the wall and opened the door.

"You are going?" he said bitterly.

"Yes." Either she could not hold seriousness long in her capricious little fancy, or, with feminine tact, she sought to make the parting less difficult for him, for she broke into a dazzling smile. "Yes, I'm goin' to run Blue Lightning agin Charley and that way bag back to Laurel Run, and break the record."

*****

It is said that she did! Perhaps owing to the fact that the grade of the return journey to Laurel Run was in her favor, and that she could avoid the long, circuitous ascent to the summit taken by the stage, or that, owing to the extraordinary difficulties in the carriage of the way bag,—which had to be twice rescued from under the wheels of the stage,—she entered the Laurel Run post-office as the coach leaders came trotting up the hill. Mr. Home was already on the platform.

"You'll have to ballast your next way bag, boss," said Charley, gravely, as it escaped his clutches once more in the dust of the road, "or you'll have to make a new contract with the company. We've lost ten minutes in five miles over that bucking thing."

Home did not reply, but quickly dragged his prize into the office, scarcely noticing Mrs. Baker, who stood beside him pale and breathless. As the bolt of the bag was drawn, revealing its chaotic interior, Mrs. Baker gave a little sigh. Home glanced quickly at her, emptied the bag upon the floor, and picked up the broken and half-filled money parcel. Then he collected the scattered coins and counted them. "It's all right, Mrs. Baker," he said gravely. "HE'S safe this time."

"I'm so glad!" said little Mrs. Baker, with a hypocritical gasp.

"So am I," returned Home, with increasing gravity, as he took the coin, "for, from all I have gathered this afternoon, it seems he was an old pioneer of Laurel Run, a friend of your husband's, and, I think, more fool than knave!" He was silent for a moment, clicking the coins against each other; then he said carelessly: "Did he get quite away, Mrs. Baker?"

"I'm sure I don't know what you're talking about," said Mrs. Baker, with a lofty air of dignity, but a somewhat debasing color. "I don't see why I should know anything about it, or why he should go away at all."

"Well," said Mr. Home, laying his hand gently on the widow's shoulder, "well, you see, it might have occurred to his friends that the COINS WERE MARKED! That is, no doubt, the reason why he would take their good advice and go. But, as I said before, Mrs. Baker, YOU'RE all right, whatever happens,—the Government stands by YOU!"

A NIGHT AT "HAYS"

CHAPTER I

It was difficult to say if Hays' farmhouse, or "Hays," as it was familiarly called, looked any more bleak and cheerless that winter afternoon than it usually did in the strong summer sunshine. Painted a cold merciless white, with scant projections for shadows, a roof of white-pine shingles, bleached lighter through sun and wind, and covered with low, white-capped chimneys, it looked even more stark and chilly than the drifts which had climbed its low roadside fence, and yet seemed hopeless of gaining a foothold on the glancing walls, or slippery, wind-swept roof. The storm, which had already heaped the hollows of the road with snow, hurled its finely-granulated flakes against the building, but they were whirled along the gutters and ridges, and disappeared in smokelike puffs across the icy roof. The granite outcrop in the hilly field beyond had long ago whitened and vanished; the dwarf firs and larches which had at first taken uncouth shapes in the drift blended vaguely together, and then merged into an unbroken formless wave. But the gaunt angles and rigid outlines of the building remained sharp and unchanged. It would seem as if the rigors of winter had only accented their hardness, as the fierceness of summer had previously made them intolerable.

It was believed that some of this unyielding grimness attached to Hays himself. Certain it is that neither hardship nor prosperity had touched his character. Years ago his emigrant team had broken down in this wild but wooded defile of the Sierras, and he had been forced to a winter encampment, with only a rude log-cabin for shelter, on the very verge of the promised land. Unable to enter it himself, he was nevertheless able to assist the better-equipped teams that followed him with wood and water and a coarse forage gathered from a sheltered slope of wild oats. This was the beginning of a rude "supply station" which afterwards became so profitable that when spring came and Hays' team were sufficiently recruited to follow the flood of immigrating gold-seekers to the placers and valleys, there seemed no occasion for it. His fortune had been already found in the belt of arable slope behind the wooded defile, and in the miraculously located coign of vantage on what was now the great highway of travel and the only oasis and first relief of the weary journey; the breaking down of his own team at that spot had not only been the salvation of those who found at "Hays" the means of prosecuting the last part of their pilgrimage, but later provided the equipment of returning teams.

The first two years of this experience had not been without hardship and danger. He had been raided by Indians and besieged for three days in his stockaded cabin; he had been invested by wintry drifts of twenty feet of snow, cut off equally from incoming teams from the pass and the valley below. During the second year his wife had joined him with four children, but whether the enforced separation had dulled her conjugal affection, or whether she was tempted by a natural feminine longing for the land of promise beyond, she sought it one morning with a fascinating teamster, leaving her two sons and two daughters behind her; two years later the elder of the daughters followed the mother's example, with such maidenly discretion, however, as to forbear compromising herself by any previous matrimonial formality whatever. From that day Hays had no further personal intercourse with the valley below. He put up a hotel a mile away from the farmhouse that he might not have to dispense hospitality to his customers, nor accept their near companionship. Always a severe Presbyterian, and an uncompromising deacon of a far-scattered and scanty community who occasionally held their service in one of his barns, he grew more rigid, sectarian, and narrow day by day. He was feared, and although neither respected nor loved, his domination and endurance were accepted. A grim landlord, hard creditor, close-fisted patron, and a smileless neighbor who neither gambled nor drank, "Old Hays," as he was called, while yet scarce fifty, had few acquaintances and fewer friends. There were those who believed that his domestic infelicities were the result of his unsympathetic nature; it never occurred to any one (but himself probably) that they might have been the cause. In those Sierran altitudes, as elsewhere, the belief in original sin—popularly known as "pure cussedness"—dominated and overbore any consideration of passive, impelling circumstances or temptation, unless they had been actively demonstrated with a revolver. The passive expression of harshness, suspicion, distrust, and moroseness was looked upon as inherent wickedness.

The storm raged violently as Hays emerged from the last of a long range of outbuildings and sheds, and crossed the open space between him and the farmhouse. Before he had reached the porch, with its scant shelter, he had floundered through a snowdrift, and faced the full fury of the storm. But the snow seemed to have glanced from his hard angular figure as it had from his roof-ridge, for when he entered the narrow hall-way his pilot jacket was unmarked, except where a narrow line of powdered flakes outlined the seams as if worn. To the right was an apartment, half office, half sitting-room, furnished with a dark and chilly iron safe, a sofa and chairs covered with black and coldly shining horsehair. Here Hays not only removed his upper coat but his under one also, and drawing a chair before the fire sat down in his shirt-sleeves. It was his usual rustic pioneer habit, and might have been some lingering reminiscence of certain remote ancestors to whom clothes were an impediment. He was warming his hands and placidly ignoring his gaunt arms in their thinly-clad "hickory" sleeves, when a young girl of eighteen sauntered, half perfunctorily, half inquisitively into the room. It was his only remaining daughter. Already elected by circumstances to a dry household virginity, her somewhat large features, sallow complexion, and tasteless, unattractive dress, did not obviously suggest a sacrifice. Since her sister's departure she had taken sole charge of her father's domestic affairs and the few rude servants he employed, with a certain inherited following of his own moods and methods. To the neighbors she was known as "Miss Hays,"—a dubious respect that, in a community of familiar "Sallies," "Mamies," "Pussies," was grimly prophetic. Yet she rejoiced in the Oriental appellation of "Zuleika." To this it is needless to add that it was impossible to conceive any one who looked more decidedly Western.

"Ye kin put some things in my carpet bag agin the time the sled comes round," said her father meditatively, without looking up.

"Then you're not coming back tonight?" asked the girl curiously. "What's goin' on at the summit, father?"

"I am," he said grimly. "You don't reckon I kalkilate to stop thar! I'm going on as far as Horseley's to close up that contract afore the weather changes."

"I kinder allowed it was funny you'd go to the hotel to-night.

There's a dance there; those two Wetherbee girls and Mamie Harris passed up the road an hour ago on a wood-sled, nigh blown to pieces and sittin' up in the snow like skeert white rabbits."

Hays' brow darkened heavily.

"Let 'em go," he said, in a hard voice that the fire did not seem to have softened. "Let 'em go for all the good their fool-parents will ever get outer them, or the herd of wayside cattle they've let them loose among.

"I reckon they haven't much to do at home, or are hard put for company, to travel six miles in the snow to show off their prinkin' to a lot of idle louts shiny with bear's grease and scented up with doctor's stuff," added the girl, shrugging her shoulders, with a touch of her father's mood and manner.

Perhaps it struck Hays at that moment that her attitude was somewhat monstrous and unnatural for one still young and presumably like other girls, for, after glancing at her under his heavy brows, he said, in a gentler tone:—

"Never YOU mind, Zuly. When your brother Jack comes home he'll know what's what, and have all the proper New York ways and style. It's nigh on three years now that he's had the best training Dr. Dawson's Academy could give,—sayin' nothing of the pow'ful Christian example of one of the best preachers in the States. They mayn't have worldly, ungodly fandangoes where he is, and riotous livin', and scarlet abominations, but I've been told that they've 'tea circles,' and 'assemblies,' and 'harmony concerts' of young folks—and dancin'—yes, fine square dancin' under control. No, I ain't stinted him in anythin'. You kin remember that, Zuleika, when you hear any more gossip and backbitin' about your father's meanness. I ain't spared no money for him."

"I reckon not," said the girl, a little sharply. "Why, there's that draft fur two hundred and fifty dollars that kem only last week from the Doctor's fur extras."

"Yes," replied Hays, with a slight knitting of the brows, "the Doctor mout hev writ more particklers, but parsons ain't allus business men. I reckon these here extrys were to push Jack along in the term, as the Doctor knew I wanted him back here in the spring, now that his brother has got to be too stiff-necked and self-opinionated to do his father's work." It seemed from this that there had been a quarrel between Hays and his eldest son, who conducted his branch business at Sacramento, and who had in a passion threatened to set up a rival establishment to his father's. And it was also evident from the manner of the girl that she was by no means a strong partisan of her father in the quarrel.

"You'd better find out first how all the schoolin' and trainin' of Jack's is goin' to jibe with the Ranch, and if he ain't been eddicated out of all knowledge of station business or keer for it. New York ain't Hays' Ranch, and these yer 'assemblies' and 'harmony' doin's and their airs and graces may put him out of conceit with our plain ways. I reckon ye didn't take that to mind when you've been hustlin' round payin' two hundred and fifty dollar drafts for Jack and quo'llin' with Bijah! I ain't sayin' nothin', father, only mebbe if Bijah had had drafts and extrys flourished around him a little more, mebbe he'd have been more polite and not so rough spoken. Mebbe," she continued with a little laugh, "even I'D be a little more in the style to suit Master Jack when he comes ef I had three hundred dollars' worth of convent schoolin' like Mamie Harris."

"Yes, and you'd have only made yourself fair game for ev'ry schemin', lazy sport or counter-jumper along the road from this to Sacramento!" responded Hays savagely.

Zuleika laughed again constrainedly, but in a way that might have suggested that this dreadful contingency was still one that it was possible to contemplate without entire consternation. As she moved slowly towards the door she stopped, with her hand on the lock, and said tentatively: "I reckon you won't be wantin' any supper before you go? You're almost sure to be offered suthin' up at Horseley's, while if I have to cook you up suthin' now and still have the men's regular supper to get at seven, it makes all the expense of an extra meal."

Hays hesitated. He would have preferred his supper now, and had his daughter pressed him would have accepted it. But economy, which was one of Zuleika's inherited instincts, vaguely appearing to him to be a virtue, interchangeable with chastity and abstemiousness, was certainly to be encouraged in a young girl. It hardly seems possible that with an eye single to the integrity of the larder she could ever look kindly on the blandishments of his sex, or, indeed, be exposed to them. He said simply: "Don't cook for me," and resumed his attitude before the fire as the girl left the room.

As he sat there, grim and immovable as one of the battered fire-dogs before him, the wind in the chimney seemed to carry on a deep-throated, dejected, and confidential conversation with him, but really had very little to reveal. There were no haunting reminiscences of his married life in this room, which he had always occupied in preference to the company or sitting-room beyond. There were no familiar shadows of the past lurking in its corners to pervade his reverie. When he did reflect, which was seldom, there was always in his mind a vague idea of a central injustice to which he had been subjected, that was to be avoided by circuitous movement, to be hidden by work, but never to be surmounted. And to-night he was going out in the storm, which he could understand and fight, as he had often done before, and he was going to drive a bargain with a man like himself and get the better of him if he could, as he had done before, and another day would be gone, and that central injustice which he could not understand would be circumvented, and he would still be holding his own in the world. And the God of Israel whom he believed in, and who was a hard but conscientious Providence, something like himself, would assist him perhaps some day to the understanding of this same vague injustice which He was, for some strange reason, permitting. But never more unrelenting and unsparing of others than when under conviction of Sin himself, and never more harsh and unforgiving than when fresh from the contemplation of the Divine Mercy, he still sat there grimly holding his hand to a warmth that never seemed to get nearer his heart than that, when his daughter re-entered the room with his carpet-bag.

To rise, put on his coat and overcoat, secure a fur cap on his head by a woolen comforter, covering his ears and twined round his throat, and to rigidly offer a square and weather-beaten cheek to his daughter's dusty kiss, did not, apparently, suggest any lingering or hesitation. The sled was at the door, which, for a tumultuous moment, opened on the storm and the white vision of a horse knee-deep in a drift, and then closed behind him. Zuleika shot the bolt, brushed some flakes of the invading snow from the mat, and, after frugally raking down the fire on the hearth her father had just quitted, retired through the long passage to the kitchen and her domestic supervision.

It was a few hours later, supper had long past; the "hands" had one by one returned to their quarters under the roof or in the adjacent lofts, and Zuleika and the two maids had at last abandoned the kitchen for their bedrooms beyond. Zuleika herself, by the light of a solitary candle, had entered the office and had dropped meditatively into a chair, as she slowly raked the warm ashes over the still smouldering fire. The barking of dogs had momentarily attracted her attention, but it had suddenly ceased. It was followed, however, by a more startling incident,—a slight movement outside, and an attempt to raise the window!

She was not frightened; perhaps there was little for her to fear; it was known that Hays kept no money in the house, the safe was only used for securities and contracts, and there were half a dozen men within call. It was, therefore, only her usual active, burning curiosity for novel incident that made her run to the window and peer out; but it was with a spontaneous cry of astonishment she turned and darted to the front door, and opened it to the muffled figure of a young man.

"Jack! Saints alive! Why, of all things!" she gasped, incoherently.

He stopped her with an impatient gesture and a hand that prevented her from closing the door again.

"Dad ain't here?" he asked quickly.

"No."

"When'll he be back?"

"Not to-night."

"Good," he said, turning to the door again. She could see a motionless horse and sleigh in the road, with a woman holding the reins.

He beckoned to the woman, who drove to the door and jumped out. Tall, handsome, and audacious, she looked at

Zuleika with a quick laugh of confidence, as at some recognized absurdity.

"Go in there," said the young man, opening the door of the office; "I'll come back in a minute."

As she entered, still smiling, as if taking part in some humorous but risky situation, he turned quickly to Zuleika and said in a low voice: "Where can we talk?"

The girl held out her hand and glided hurriedly through the passage until she reached a door, which she opened. By the light of a dying fire he could see it was her bedroom. Lighting a candle on the mantel, she looked eagerly in his face as he threw aside his muffler and opened his coat. It disclosed a spare, youthful figure, and a thin, weak face that a budding mustache only seemed to make still more immature. For an instant brother and sister gazed at each other. Astonishment on her part, nervous impatience on his, apparently repressed any demonstration of family affection. Yet when she was about to speak he stopped her roughly.

"There now; don't talk. I know what you're goin' to say—could say it myself if I wanted to—and it's no use. Well then, here I am. You saw HER. Well, she's MY WIFE—we've been married three months. Yes, my WIFE; married three months ago. I'm here because I ran away from school—that is, I HAVEN'T BEEN THERE for the last three months. I came out with her last steamer; we went up to the Summit Hotel last night—where they didn't know me—until we could see how the land lay, before popping down on dad. I happened to learn that he was out to-night, and I brought her down here to have a talk. We can go back again before he comes, you know, unless"—

"But," interrupted the girl, with sudden practicality, "you say you ain't been at Doctor Dawson's for three months! Why, only last week he drew on dad for two hundred and fifty dollars for your extras!"

He glanced around him and then arranged his necktie in the glass above the mantel with a nervous laugh.

"OH, THAT! I fixed that up, and got the money for it in New York to pay our passage with. It's all right, you know."

CHAPTER II

The girl stood looking at the ingenious forger with an odd, breathless smile. It was difficult to determine, however, if gratified curiosity were not its most dominant expression.

"And you've got a wife—and THAT'S her?" she resumed.

"Yes."

"Where did you first meet her? Who is she?"

"She's an actress—mighty popular in 'Frisco—I mean New York. Lot o' chaps tried to get her—I cut 'em out. For all dad's trying to keep me at Dawson's—I ain't such a fool, eh?"

Nevertheless, as he stood there stroking his fair mustache, his astuteness did not seem to impress his sister to enthusiastic assent. Yet she did not relax her breathless, inquisitive smile as she went on:—

"And what are you going to do about dad?"

He turned upon her querulously.

"Well, that's what I want to talk about."

"You'll catch it!" she said impressively. But here her brother's nervousness broke out into a weak, impotent fury. It was evident, too, that in spite of its apparent spontaneous irritation its intent was studied. Catch it! Would he? Oh, yes! Well, she'd see WHO'D catch it! Not him. No, he'd had enough of this meanness, and wanted it ended! He wasn't a woman to be treated like his sister,—like their mother—like their brother, if it came to that, for he knew how he was to be brought back to take Bijah's place in the spring; he'd heard the whole story. No, he was going to stand up for his rights,—he was going to be treated as the son of a man who was worth half a million ought to be treated! He wasn't going to be skimped, while his father was wallowing in money that he didn't know what to do with,—money that by rights ought to have been given to their mother and their sister. Why, even the law wouldn't permit such meanness—if he was dead. No, he'd come back with Lottie, his wife, to show his father that there was one of the family that couldn't be fooled and bullied, and wouldn't put up with it any longer. There was going to be a fair division of the property, and his sister Annie's property, and hers—Zuleika's—too, if she'd have the pluck to speak up for herself. All this and much more he said. Yet even while his small fury was genuine and characteristic, there was such an evident incongruity between himself and his speech that it seemed to fit him loosely, and in a measure flapped in his gestures like another's garment. Zuleika, who had exhibited neither disgust nor sympathy with his rebellion, but had rather appeared to enjoy it as a novel domestic performance, the morality of which devolved solely upon the performer, retained her curious smile. And then a knock at the door startled them.

It was the stranger,—slightly apologetic and still humorous, but firm and self-confident withal. She was sorry to interrupt their family council, but the fire was going out where she sat, and she would like a cup of tea or some refreshment. She did not look at Jack, but, completely ignoring him, addressed herself to Zuleika with what seemed to be a direct challenge; in that feminine eye-grapple there was a quick, instinctive, and final struggle between the two women. The stranger triumphed. Zuleika's vacant smile changed to one of submission, and then, equally ignoring her brother in this double defeat, she hastened to the kitchen to do the visitor's bidding. The woman closed the door behind her, and took

Zuleika's place before the fire.

"Well?" she said, in a half-contemptuous toleration.

"Well?" said Jack, in an equally ill-disguised discontent, but an evident desire to placate the woman before him. "It's all right, you know. I've had my say. It'll come right, Lottie, you'll see."

The woman smiled again, and glanced around the bare walls of the room.

"And I suppose," she said, drily, "when it comes right I'm to take the place of your sister in the charge of this workhouse and succeed to the keys of that safe in the other room?"

"It'll come all right, I tell you; you can fix things up here any way you'll like when we get the old man straight," said Jack, with the iteration of feebleness. "And as to that safe, I've seen it chock full of securities."

"It'll hold one less to-night," she said, looking at the fire.

"What are you talking about?" he asked, in querulous suspicion.

She drew a paper from her pocket.

"It's that draft of yours that you were crazy enough to sign Dawson's name to. It was lying out there on the desk. I reckon it isn't a thing you care to have kept as evidence, even by your father."

She held it in the flames until it was consumed.

"By Jove, your head is level, Lottie!" he said, with an

admiration that was not, however, without a weak reserve of suspicion.

"No, it isn't, or I wouldn't be here," she said, curtly. Then she added, as if dismissing the subject, "Well, what did you tell her?"

"Oh, I said I met you in New York. You see I thought she might think it queer if she knew I only met you in San Francisco three weeks ago. Of course I said we were married."

She looked at him with weary astonishment.

"And of course, whether things go right or not, she'll find out that I've got a husband living, that I never met you in New York, but on the steamer, and that you've lied. I don't see the USE of it. You said you were going to tell the whole thing squarely and say the truth, and that's why I came to help you."

"Yes; but don't you see, hang it all!" he stammered, in the irritation of weak confusion, "I had to tell her SOMETHING. Father won't dare to tell her the truth, no more than he will the neighbors. He'll hush it up, you bet; and when we get this thing fixed you'll go and get your divorce, you know, and we'll be married privately on the square."

He looked so vague, so immature, yet so fatuously self-confident, that the woman extended her hand with a laugh and tapped him on the back as she might have patted a dog. Then she disappeared to follow Zuleika in the kitchen.

When the two women returned together they were evidently on the best of terms. So much so that the man, with the easy reaction of a shallow nature, became sanguine and exalted, even to an ostentatious exhibition of those New York graces on which the paternal Hays had set such store. He complacently explained the methods by which he had deceived Dr. Dawson; how he had himself written a letter from his father commanding him to return to take his brother's place, and how he had shown it to the Doctor and been three months in San Francisco looking for work and assisting Lottie at the theatre, until a conviction of the righteousness of his cause, perhaps combined with the fact that they were also short of money and she had no engagement, impelled him to his present heroic step. All of which Zuleika listened to with childish interest, but superior appreciation of his companion. The fact that this woman was an actress, an abomination vaguely alluded to by her father as being even more mysteriously wicked than her sister and mother, and correspondingly exciting, as offering a possible permanent relief to the monotony of her home life, seemed to excuse her brother's weakness. She was almost ready to become his partisan—AFTER she had seen her father.

They had talked largely of their plans; they had settled small details of the future and the arrangement of the property; they had agreed that Zuleika should be relieved of her household drudgery, and sent to a fashionable school in San Francisco with a music teacher and a dressmaker. They had discussed everything but the precise manner in which the revelation should be conveyed to Hays. There was still plenty of time for that, for he would not return until to-morrow at noon, and it was already tacitly understood that the vehicle of transmission should be a letter from the Summit Hotel. The possible contingency of a sudden outburst of human passion not entirely controlled by religious feeling was to be guarded against.

They were sitting comfortably before the replenished fire; the wind was still moaning in the chimney, when, suddenly, in a lull of the storm the sound of sleigh-bells seemed to fill the room. It was followed by a voice from without, and, with a hysterical cry, Zuleika started to her feet. The same breathless smile with which she had greeted her brother an hour ago was upon her lips as she gasped:—

"Lord, save us!—but it's dad come back!"

I grieve to say that here the doughty redresser of domestic wrongs and retriever of the family honor lapsed white-faced in his chair idealess and tremulous. It was his frailer companion who rose to the occasion and even partly dragged him with her. "Go back to the hotel," she said quickly, "and take the sled with you,—you are not fit to face him now! But he does not know ME, and I will stay!" To the staring Zuleika: "I am a stranger stopped by a broken sleigh on my way to the hotel. Leave the rest to me. Now clear out, both of you. I'll let him in."

She looked so confident, self-contained, and superior, that the thought of opposition never entered their minds, and as an impatient rapping rose from the door they let her, with a half-impatient, half-laughing gesture, drive them before her from the room. When they had disappeared in the distance, she turned to the front door, unbolted and opened it. Hays blundered in out of the snow with a muttered exclamation, and then, as the light from the open office door revealed a stranger, started and fell back.

"Miss Hays is busy," said the woman quietly, "I am afraid, on my account. But my sleigh broke down on the way to the hotel and I was forced to get out here. I suppose this is Mr. Hays?"

A strange woman—by her dress and appearance a very worldling—and even braver in looks and apparel than many he had seen in the cities—seemed, in spite of all his precautions, to have fallen short of the hotel and been precipitated upon him! Yet under the influence of some odd abstraction he was affected by it less than he could have believed. He even achieved a rude bow as he bolted the door and ushered her into the office. More than that, he found himself explaining to the fair trespasser the reasons of his return to his own home. For, like a direct man, he had a consciousness of some inconsistency in his return—or in the circumstances that induced a change of plans which might conscientiously require an explanation.

"You see, ma'am, a rather singular thing happened to me after I passed the summit. Three times I lost the track, got off it somehow, and found myself traveling in a circle. The third time, when I struck my own tracks again, I concluded I'd just follow them back here. I suppose I might have got the road again by tryin' and fightin' the snow—but ther's some things not worth the fightin'. This was a matter of business, and, after all, ma'am, business ain't everythin', is it?"

He was evidently in some unusual mood, the mood that with certain reticent natures often compels them to make their brief confidences to utter strangers rather than impart them to those intimate friends who might remind them of their weakness. She agreed with him pleasantly, but not so obviously as to excite suspicion. "And you preferred to let your business go, and come back to the comfort of your own home and family."

"The comfort of my home and family?" he repeated in a dry, deliberate voice. "Well, I reckon I ain't been tempted much by THAT. That isn't what I meant." But he went back to the phrase, repeating it grimly, as if it were some mandatory text. "The comfort of my OWN HOME AND FAMILY! Well, Satan hasn't set THAT trap for my feet yet, ma'am. No;

ye saw my daughter? well, that's all my family; ye see this room? that's all my home. My wife ran away from me; my daughter cleared out too, my eldest son as was with me here has quo'lled with me and reckons to set up a rival business agin me. No," he said, still more meditatively and deliberately; "it wasn't to come back to the comforts of my own home and family that I faced round on Heavy Tree Hill, I reckon."

As the woman, for certain reasons, had no desire to check this auspicious and unlooked for confidence, she waited patiently. Hays remained silent for an instant, warming his hands before the fire, and then looked up interrogatively.

"A professor of religion, ma'am, or under conviction?"

"Not exactly," said the lady smiling.

"Excuse me, but in spite of your fine clothes I reckoned you had a serious look just now. A reader of Scripture, may be?"

"I know the Bible."

"You remember when the angel with the flamin' sword appeared unto Saul on the road to Damascus?"

"Yes."

"It mout hev been suthin' in that style that stopped me," he said slowly and tentatively. "Though nat'rally I didn't SEE anything, and only had the queer feelin'. It might hev been THAT shied my mare off the track."

"But Saul was up to some wickedness, wasn't he?" said the lady smilingly, "while YOU were simply going somewhere on business?"

"Yes," said Hays thoughtfully, "but my BUSINESS might hev seemed like persecution. I don't mind tellin' you what it was if you'd care to listen. But mebbe you're tired. Mebbe you want to retire. You know," he went on with a sudden hospitable outburst, "you needn't be in any hurry to go; we kin take care of you here to-night, and it'll cost you nothin'. And I'll send you on with my sleigh in the mornin'. Per'aps you'd like suthin' to eat—a cup of tea—or—I'll call Zuleika;" and he rose with an expression of awkward courtesy.

But the lady, albeit with a self-satisfied sparkle in her dark eyes, here carelessly assured him that Zuleika had already given her refreshment, and, indeed, was at that moment preparing her own room for her. She begged he would not interrupt his interesting story.

Hays looked relieved.

"Well, I reckon I won't call her, for what I was goin' to say ain't exackly the sort o' thin' for an innocent, simple sort o' thing like her to hear—I mean," he interrupted himself hastily—"that folks of more experience of the world like you and me don't mind speakin' of—I'm sorter takin' it for granted that you're a married woman, ma'am."

The lady, who had regarded him with a sudden rigidity, here relaxed her expression and nodded.

"Well," continued Hays, resuming his place by the fire, "you see this yer man I was goin' to see lives about four miles beyond the summit on a ranch that furnishes most of the hay for the stock that side of the Divide. He's bin holdin' off his next year's contracts with me, hopin' to make better terms from the prospects of a late spring and higher prices. He held his head mighty high and talked big of waitin' his own time. I happened to know he couldn't do it."

He put his hands on his knees and stared at the fire, and then went on:—

"Ye see this man had had crosses and family trials. He had a wife that left him to jine a lot of bally dancers and painted women in the 'Frisco playhouses when he was livin' in the southern country. You'll say that was like MY own case,—and mebbe that was why it came to him to tell me about it,—but the difference betwixt HIM and ME was that instead of restin' unto the Lord and findin' Him, and pluckin' out the eye that offended him 'cordin' to Scripter, as I did, HE followed after HER tryin' to get her back, until, findin' that wasn't no use, he took a big disgust and came up here to hide hisself, where there wasn't no playhouse nor play-actors, and no wimmen but Injin squaws. He pre-empted the land, and nat'rally, there bein' no one ez cared to live there but himself, he had it all his own way, made it pay, and, as I was sayin' before, held his head high for prices. Well—you ain't gettin' tired, ma'am?"

"No," said the lady, resting her cheek on her hand and gazing on the fire, "it's all very interesting; and so odd that you two men, with nearly the same experiences, should be neighbors."

"Say buyer and seller, ma'am, not neighbors—at least Scrip-toorily—nor friends. Well,—now this is where the Speshal Providence comes in,—only this afternoon Jim Briggs, hearin' me speak of Horseley's offishness"—

"WHOSE offishness?" asked the lady.

"Horseley's offishness,—Horseley's the name of the man I'm talkin' about. Well, hearin' that, he says: 'You hold on, Hays, and he'll climb down. That wife of his has left the stage—got sick of it—and is driftin' round in 'Frisco with some fellow.

When Horseley gets to hear that, you can't keep him here,—he'll settle up, sell out, and realize on everything he's got to go after her agin,—you bet.' That's what Briggs said. Well, that's what sent me up to Horseley's to-night—to get there, drop the news, and then pin him down to that contract."

"It looked like a good stroke of business and a fair one," said the lady in an odd voice. It was so odd that Hays looked up. But she had somewhat altered her position, and was gazing at the ceiling, and with her hand to her face seemed to have just recovered from a slight yawn, at which he hesitated with a new and timid sense of politeness.

"You're gettin' tired, ma'am?"

"Oh dear, no!" she said in the same voice, but clearing her throat with a little cough. "And why didn't you see this Mr. Horseley after all? Oh, I forgot!—you said you changed your mind from something you'd heard."

He had turned his eyes to the fire again, but without noticing as he did so that she slowly moved her face, still half hidden by her hand, towards him and was watching him intently.

"No," he said, slowly, "nothin' I heard, somethin' I felt. It mout hev been that that set me off the track. It kem to me all of a sudden that he might be sittin' thar calm and peaceful like ez I might be here, hevin' forgot all about her and his trouble, and here was me goin' to drop down upon him and start it all fresh agin. It looked a little like persecution—yes, like persecution. I got rid of it, sayin' to myself it was business. But I'd got off the road meantime, and had to find it again, and whenever I got back to the track and was pointed for his house, it all seemed to come back on me and set me off agin. When that had happened three times, I turned round and started for home."

"And do you mean to say," said the lady, with a discordant laugh, "that you believe, because YOU didn't go there and break the news, that nobody else will? That he won't hear of it from the first man he meets?"

"He don't meet any one up where he lives, and only Briggs and myself know it, and I'll see that Briggs don't tell. But it was mighty queer this whole thing comin' upon me suddenly,—wasn't it?"

"Very queer," replied the lady; "for"—with the same metallic laugh—"you don't seem to be given to this kind of weakness with your own family."

If there was any doubt as to the sarcastic suggestion of her voice, there certainly could be none in the wicked glitter of her eyes fixed upon his face under her shading hand. But haply he seemed unconscious of both, and even accepted her statement without an ulterior significance.

"Yes," he said, communingly, to the glaring embers of the hearth, "it must have been a special revelation."

There was something so fatuous and one-idea'd in his attitude and expression, so monstrously inconsistent and inadequate to what was going on around him, and so hopelessly stupid—if a mere simulation—that the angry suspicion that he was acting a part slowly faded from her eyes, and a hysterical smile began to twitch her set lips. She still gazed at him. The wind howled drearily in the chimney; all that was economic, grim, and cheerless in the room seemed to gather as flitting shadows around that central figure. Suddenly she arose with such a quick rustling of her skirts that he lifted his eyes with a start; for she was standing immediately before him, her hands behind her, her handsome, audacious face bent smilingly forward, and her bold, brilliant eyes within a foot of his own.

"Now, Mr. Hays, do you want to know what this warning or special revelation of yours REALLY meant? Well, it had nothing whatever to do with that man on the summit. No. The whole interest, gist, and meaning of it was simply this, that you should turn round and come straight back here and"—she drew back and made him an exaggerated theatrical curtsey—"have the supreme pleasure of making MY acquaintance! That was all. And now, as you've HAD IT, in five minutes I must be off. You've offered me already your horse and sleigh to go to the summit. I accept it and go! Good-by!"

He knew nothing of a woman's coquettish humor; he knew still less of that mimic stage from which her present voice, gesture, and expression were borrowed; he had no knowledge of the burlesque emotions which that voice, gesture, and expression were supposed to portray, and finally and fatally he was unable to detect the feminine hysteric jar and discord that underlay it all. He thought it was strong, characteristic, and real, and accepted it literally. He rose.

"Ef you allow you can't stay, why I'll go and get the horse. I reckon he ain't bin put up yet."

"Do, please."

He grimly resumed his coat and hat and disappeared through the passage into the kitchen, whence, a moment later, Zuleika came flying.

"Well, what has happened?" she said eagerly.

"It's all right," said the woman quickly, "though he knows nothing yet. But I've got things fixed generally, so that he'll be quite ready to have it broken to him by this time to-morrow. But don't you say anything till I've seen Jack and you hear from HIM. Remember."

She spoke rapidly; her cheeks were quite glowing from some sudden energy; so were Zuleika's with the excitement of curiosity. Presently the sound of sleigh-bells again filled the room. It was Hays leading the horse and sleigh to the door, beneath a sky now starlit and crisp under a northeast wind. The fair stranger cast a significant glance at Zuleika, and whispered hurriedly, "You know he must not come with me. You must keep him here."

She ran to the door muffled and hooded, leaped into the sleigh, and gathered up the reins.

"But you cannot go alone," said Hays, with awkward courtesy. "I was kalkilatin'"—

"You're too tired to go out again, dad," broke in Zuleika's voice quickly. "You ain't fit; you're all gray and krinkly now, like as when you had one of your last spells. She'll send the sleigh back to-morrow."

"I can find my way," said the lady briskly; "there's only one turn off, I believe, and that"—

"Leads to the stage station three miles west. You needn't be afraid of gettin' off on that, for you'll likely see the down stage crossin' your road ez soon ez you get clear of the ranch."

"Good-night," said the lady. An arc of white spray sprang before the forward runner, and the sleigh vanished in the road.

Father and daughter returned to the office.

"You didn't get to know her, dad, did ye?" queried Zuleika.

"No," responded Hays gravely, "except to see she wasn't no backwoods or mountaineering sort. Now, there's the kind of woman, Zuly, as knows her own mind and yours too; that a man like your brother Jack oughter pick out when he marries."

Zuleika's face beamed behind her father. "You ain't goin' to sit up any longer, dad?" she said, as she noticed him resume his seat by the fire. "It's gettin' late, and you look mighty tuckered out with your night's work."

"Do you know what she said, Zuly?" returned her father, after a pause, which turned out to have been a long, silent laugh.

"No."

"She said," he repeated slowly, "that she reckoned I came back here to-night to have the pleasure of her acquaintance!" He brought his two hands heavily down upon his knees, rubbing them down deliberately towards his ankles, and leaning forward with his face to the fire and a long-sustained smile of complete though tardy appreciation.

He was still in this attitude when Zuleika left him. The wind crooned over him confidentially, but he still sat there, given up apparently to some posthumous enjoyment of his visitor's departing witticism.

It was scarcely daylight when Zuleika, while dressing, heard a quick tapping upon her shutter. She opened it to the scared and bewildered face of her brother.

"What happened with her and father last night?" he said hoarsely.

"Nothing—why?"

"Read that. It was brought to me half an hour ago by a man in dad's sleigh, from the stage station."

He handed her a crumpled note with trembling fingers. She took it and read:—

"The game's up and I'm out of it! Take my advice and clear out of it too, until you can come back in better shape. Don't be such a fool as to try and follow me. Your father isn't one, and that's where you've slipped up."

"He shall pay for it, whatever he's done," said her brother with an access of wild passion. "Where is he?"

"Why, Jack, you wouldn't dare to see him now?"

"Wouldn't I?" He turned and ran, convulsed with passion, before the windows towards the front of the house. Zuleika slipped out of her bedroom and ran to her father's room. He was not there. Already she could hear her brother hammering frantically against the locked front door.

The door of the office was partly open. Her father was still there. Asleep? Yes, for he had apparently sunk forward before the cold hearth. But the hands that he had always been trying to warm were colder than the hearth or ashes, and he himself never again spoke nor stirred.

*****

It was deemed providential by the neighbors that his

youngest and favorite son, alarmed by news of his father's failing health, had arrived from the Atlantic States just at the last moment. But it was thought singular that after the division of the property he entirely abandoned the Ranch, and that even pending the division his beautiful but fastidious Eastern bride declined to visit it with her husband.

JOHNSON'S "OLD WOMAN"

It was growing dark, and the Sonora trail was becoming more indistinct before me at every step. The difficulty had increased over the grassy slope, where the overflow from some smaller watercourse above had worn a number of diverging gullies so like the trail as to be undistinguishable from it. Unable to determine which was the right one, I threw the reins over the mule's neck and resolved to trust to that superior animal's sagacity, of which I had heard so much. But I had not taken into account the equally well-known weaknesses of sex and species, and Chu Chu had already shown uncontrollable signs of wanting her own way. Without a moment's hesitation, feeling the relaxed bridle, she lay down and rolled over.

In this perplexity the sound of horse's hoofs ringing out of the rocky canyon beyond was a relief, even if momentarily embarrassing. An instant afterwards a horse and rider appeared cantering round the hill on what was evidently the lost trail, and pulled up as I succeeded in forcing Chu Chu to her legs again.

"Is that the trail from Sonora?" I asked.

"Yes;" but with a critical glance at the mule, "I reckon you ain't going thar tonight."

"Why not?"

"It's a matter of eighteen miles, and most of it a blind trail through the woods after you take the valley."

"Is it worse than this?"

"What's the matter with this trail? Ye ain't expecting a racecourse or a shell road over the foothills—are ye?"

"No. Is there any hotel where I can stop?"

"Nary."

"Nor any house?"

"No."

"Thank you. Good-night."

He had already passed on, when he halted again and turned in his saddle. "Look yer. Just a spell over yon canyon ye'll find a patch o' buckeyes; turn to the right and ye'll see a trail. That'll take ye to a shanty. You ask if it's Johnson's."

"Who's Johnson?"

"I am. You ain't lookin' for Vanderbilt or God Almighty up here, are you? Well, then, you hark to me, will you? You say to my old woman to give you supper and a shakedown somewhar to-night. Say I sent you. So long."

He was gone before I could accept or decline. An extraordinary noise proceeded from Chu Chu, not unlike a suppressed chuckle. I looked sharply at her; she coughed affectedly, and, with her head and neck stretched to their greatest length, appeared to contemplate her neat little off fore shoe with admiring abstraction. But as soon as I had mounted she set off abruptly, crossed the rocky canyon, apparently sighted the patch of buckeyes of her own volition, and without the slightest hesitation found the trail to the right, and in half an hour stood before the shanty.

It was a log cabin with an additional "lean-to" of the same material, roofed with bark, and on the other side a larger and more ambitious "extension" built of rough, unplaned, and unpainted redwood boards, lightly shingled. The "lean-to" was evidently used as a kitchen, and the central cabin as a living-room. The barking of a dog as I approached called four children of different sizes to the open door, where already an enterprising baby was feebly essaying to crawl over a bar of wood laid across the threshold to restrain it.

"Is this Johnson's house?"

My remark was really addressed to the eldest, a boy of apparently nine or ten, but I felt that my attention was unduly fascinated by the baby, who at that moment had toppled over the bar, and was calmly eyeing me upside down, while silently and heroically suffocating in its petticoats. The boy disappeared without replying, but presently returned with a taller girl of fourteen or fifteen. I was struck with the way that, as she reached the door, she passed her hands rapidly over the heads of the others as if counting them, picked up the baby, reversed it, shook out its clothes, and returned it to the inside, without even looking at it. The act was evidently automatic and habitual.

I repeated my question timidly.

Yes, it WAS Johnson's, but he had just gone to King's Mills. I replied, hurriedly, that I knew it,—that I had met him beyond the canyon. As I had lost my way and couldn't get to Sonora to-night, he had been good enough to say that I might stay there until morning. My voice was slightly raised for the benefit of Mr. Johnson's "old woman," who, I had no doubt, was inspecting me furtively from some corner.

The girl drew the children away, except the boy. To him she said simply, "Show the stranger whar to stake out his mule, 'Dolphus," and disappeared in the "extension" without another word. I followed my little guide, who was perhaps more actively curious, but equally unresponsive. To my various questions he simply returned a smile of exasperating vacuity. But he never took his eager eyes from me, and I was satisfied that not a detail of my appearance escaped him. Leading the way behind the house to a little wood, whose only "clearing" had been effected by decay or storm, he stood silently apart while I picketed Chu Chu, neither offering to assist me nor opposing any interruption to my survey of the locality. There was no trace of human cultivation in the surroundings of the cabin; the wilderness still trod sharply on the heels of the pioneer's fresh footprints, and even seemed to obliterate them. For a few yards around the actual dwelling there was an unsavory fringe of civilization in the shape of cast-off clothes, empty bottles, and tin cans, and the adjacent thorn and elder bushes blossomed unwholesomely with bits of torn white paper and bleaching dish-cloths. This hideous circle never widened; Nature always appeared to roll back the intruding debris; no bird nor beast carried it away; no animal ever forced the uncleanly barrier; civilization remained grimly trenched in its own exuvia. The old terrifying girdle of fire around the hunter's camp was not more deterring to curious night prowlers than this coarse and accidental outwork.

When I regained the cabin I found it empty, the doors of the lean-to and extension closed, but there was a stool set before a rude table, upon which smoked a tin cup of coffee, a tin dish of hot saleratus biscuit, and a plate of fried beef. There was something odd and depressing in this silent exclusion of my presence. Had Johnson's "old woman" from some dark post of observation taken a dislike to my appearance, or was this churlish withdrawal a peculiarity of Sierran hospitality? Or was Mrs. Johnson young and pretty, and hidden under the restricting ban of Johnson's jealousy, or was she a deformed cripple, or even a bedridden crone? From the extension at times came a murmur of voices, but never the accents of adult womanhood. The gathering darkness, relieved only by a dull glow from the smouldering logs in the adobe chimney, added to my loneliness. In the circumstances I knew I ought to have put aside the repast and given myself up to gloomy and pessimistic reflection; but Nature is often inconsistent, and in that keen mountain air, I grieve to say, my physical and moral condition was not in that perfect accord always indicated by romancers. I had an appetite and I gratified it; dyspepsia and ethical reflections might come later. I ate the saleratus biscuit cheerfully, and was meditatively finishing my coffee when a gurgling sound from the rafters above attracted my attention. I looked up; under the overhang of the bark roof three pairs of round eyes were fixed upon me. They belonged to the children I had previously seen, who, in the attitude of Raphael's cherubs, had evidently been deeply interested spectators of my repast. As our eyes met an inarticulate giggle escaped the lips of the youngest.

I never could understand why the shy amusement of children over their elders is not accepted as philosophically by its object as when it proceeds from an equal. We fondly believe that when Jones or Brown laughs at us it is from malice, ignorance, or a desire to show his superiority, but there is always a haunting suspicion in our minds that these little critics REALLY see something in us to laugh at. I, however, smiled affably in return, ignoring any possible grotesqueness in my manner of eating in private.

"Come here, Johnny," I said blandly.

The two elder ones, a girl and a boy, disappeared instantly, as if the crowning joke of this remark was too much for them. From a scraping and kicking against the log wall I judged that they had quickly dropped to the ground outside. The younger one, the giggler, remained fascinated, but ready to fly at a moment's warning.

"Come here, Johnny, boy," I repeated gently. "I want you to go to your mother, please, and tell her"—

But here the child, who had been working its face convulsively, suddenly uttered a lugubrious howl and disappeared also. I ran to the front door and looked out in time to see the tallest girl, who had received me, walking away with it under her arm, pushing the boy ahead of her and looking back over her shoulder, not unlike a youthful she-bear conducting her cubs from danger. She disappeared at the end of the extension, where there was evidently another door.

It was very extraordinary. It was not strange that I turned back to the cabin with a chagrin and mortification which for a moment made me entertain the wild idea of saddling Chu Chu, and shaking the dust of that taciturn house from my feet. But the ridiculousness of such an act, to say nothing of its ingratitude, as quickly presented itself to me. Johnson had offered me only food and shelter; I could have claimed no more from the inn I had asked him to direct me to. I did not re-enter the house, but, lighting my last cigar, began to walk gloomily up and down the trail. With the outcoming of the stars it had grown lighter; through a wind opening in the trees I could see the heavy bulk of the opposite mountain, and beyond it a superior crest defined by a red line of forest fire, which, however, cast no reflection on the surrounding earth or sky. Faint woodland currents of air, still warm from the afternoon sun, stirred the leaves around me with long-drawn aromatic breaths. But these in time gave way to the steady Sierran night wind sweeping down from the higher summits, and rocking the tops of the tallest pines, yet leaving the tranquillity of the dark lower aisles unshaken. It was very quiet; there was no cry nor call of beast or bird in the darkness; the long rustle of the tree-tops sounded as faint as the far-off wash of distant seas. Nor did the resemblance cease there; the close-set files of the pines and cedars, stretching in illimitable ranks to the horizon, were filled with the immeasurable loneliness of an ocean shore. In this vast silence I began to think I understood the taciturnity of the dwellers in the solitary cabin.

When I returned, however, I was surprised to find the tallest girl standing by the door. As I approached she retreated before me, and pointing to the corner where a common cot bed had been evidently just put up, said, "Ye can turn in thar, only ye'll have to rouse out early when 'Dolphus does the chores," and was turning towards the extension again, when I stopped her almost appealingly.

"One moment, please. Can I see your mother?"

She stopped and looked at me with a singular expression. Then she said sharply:—

"You know, fust rate, she's dead."

She was turning away again, but I think she must have seen my concern in my face, for she hesitated. "But," I said quickly, "I certainly understood your father, that is, Mr. Johnson," I added, interrogatively, "to say that—that I was to speak to"—I didn't like to repeat the exact phrase—

"his WIFE."

"I don't know what he was playin' ye for," she said shortly. "Mar has been dead mor'n a year."

"But," I persisted, "is there no grown-up woman here?"

"No."

"Then who takes care of you and the children?"

"I do."

"Yourself and your father—eh?"

"Dad ain't here two days running, and then on'y to sleep."

"And you take the entire charge of the house?"

"Yes, and the log tallies."

"The log tallies?"

"Yes; keep count and measure the logs that go by the slide."

It flashed upon me that I had passed the slide or declivity on the hillside, where logs were slipped down into the valley, and I inferred that Johnson's business was cutting timber for the mill.

"But you're rather young for all this work," I suggested.

"I'm goin' on sixteen," she said gravely.

Indeed, for the matter of that, she might have been any age. Her face, on which sunburn took the place of complexion, was already hard and set. But on a nearer view I was struck with the fact that her eyes, which were not large, were almost indistinguishable from the presence of the most singular eyelashes I had ever seen. Intensely black, intensely thick, and even tangled in their profusion, they bristled rather than fringed her eyelids, obliterating everything but the shining black pupils beneath, which were like certain lustrous hairy mountain berries. It was this woodland suggestion that seemed to uncannily connect her with the locality. I went on playfully:—

"That's not VERY old—but tell me—does your father, or DID your father, ever speak of you as his 'old woman?'"

She nodded. "Then you thought I was mar?" she said, smiling.

It was such a relief to see her worn face relax its expression of pathetic gravity—although this operation quite buried her eyes in their black thickest hedge again—that I continued cheerfully: "It wasn't much of a mistake, considering all you do for the house and family."

"Then you didn't tell Billy 'to go and be dead in the ground with mar,' as he 'lows you did?" she said half suspiciously, yet trembling on the edge of a smile.

No, I had not, but I admitted that my asking him to go to his mother might have been open to this dismal construction by a sensitive infant mind. She seemed mollified, and again turned to go.

"Good-night, Miss—you know your father didn't tell me your real name," I said.

"Karline!"

"Good-night, Miss Karline."

I held out my hand.

She looked at it and then at me through her intricate eyelashes. Then she struck it aside briskly, but not unkindly, said "Quit foolin', now," as she might have said to one of the children, and disappeared through the inner door. Not knowing whether to be amused or indignant, I remained silent a moment. Then I took a turn outside in the increasing darkness, listened to the now hurrying wind over the tree-tops, re-entered the cabin, closed the door, and went to bed.

But not to sleep. Perhaps the responsibility towards these solitary children, which Johnson had so lightly shaken off, devolved upon me as I lay there, for I found myself imagining a dozen emergencies of their unprotected state, with which the elder girl could scarcely grapple. There was little to fear from depredatory man or beast—desperadoes of the mountain trail never stooped to ignoble burglary, bear or panther seldom approached a cabin—but there was the chance of sudden illness, fire, the accidents that beset childhood, to say nothing of the narrowing moral and mental effect of their isolation at that tender age. It was scandalous in Johnson to leave them alone.

In the silence I found I could hear quite distinctly the sound of their voices in the extension, and it was evident that Caroline was putting them to bed. Suddenly a voice was uplifted—her own! She began to sing and the others to join her. It was the repetition of a single verse of a well-known lugubrious negro melody. "All the world am sad and dreary," wailed Caroline, in a high head-note, "everywhere I roam." "Oh, darkieth," lisped the younger girl in response, "how my heart growth weary, far from the old folkth at h-o-o-me." This was repeated two or three times before the others seemed to get the full swing of it, and then the lines rose and fell sadly and monotonously in the darkness. I don't know why, but I at once got the impression that those motherless little creatures were under a vague belief that their performance was devotional, and was really filling the place of an evening hymn. A brief and indistinct kind of recitation, followed by a dead silence, broken only by the slow creaking of new timber, as if the house were stretching itself to sleep too, confirmed my impression. Then all became quiet again.

But I was more wide awake than before. Finally I rose, dressed myself, and dragging my stool to the fire, took a book from my knapsack, and by the light of a guttering candle, which I discovered in a bottle in the corner of the hearth, began to read. Presently I fell into a doze. How long I slept I could not tell, for it seemed to me that a dreamy consciousness of a dog barking at last forced itself upon me so strongly that I awoke. The barking appeared to come from behind the cabin in the direction of the clearing where I had tethered Chu Chu. I opened the door hurriedly, ran round the cabin towards the hollow, and was almost at once met by the bulk of the frightened Chu Chu, plunging out of the darkness towards me, kept only in check by her reata in the hand of a blanketed shape slowly advancing with a gun over its shoulder out of the hollow. Before I had time to recover from my astonishment I was thrown into greater confusion by recognizing the shape as none other than Caroline!

Without the least embarrassment or even self-consciousness of her appearance, she tossed the end of the reata to me with the curtest explanation as she passed by. Some prowling bear or catamount had frightened the mule. I had better tether it before the cabin away from the wind.

"But I thought wild beasts never came so near," I said quickly.

"Mule meat's mighty temptin'," said the girl sententiously and passed on. I wanted to thank her; I wanted to say how sorry I was that she had been disturbed; I wanted to compliment her on her quiet midnight courage, and yet warn her against recklessness; I wanted to know whether she had been accustomed to such alarms; and if the gun she carried was really a necessity. But I could only respect her reticence, and I was turning away when I was struck by a more inexplicable spectacle. As she neared the end of the extension I distinctly saw the tall figure of a man, moving with a certain diffidence and hesitation that did not, however, suggest any intention of concealment, among the trees; the girl apparently saw him at the same moment and slightly slackened her pace. Not more than a dozen feet separated them. He said something that was inaudible to my ears,—but whether from his hesitation or the distance I could not determine. There was no such uncertainty in her reply, however, which was given in her usual curt fashion: "All right. You can trapse along home now and turn in."

She turned the corner of the extension and disappeared. The tall figure of the man wavered hesitatingly for a moment, and then vanished also. But I was too much excited by curiosity to accept this unsatisfactory conclusion, and, hastily picketing Chu Chu a few rods from the front door, I ran after him, with an instinctive feeling that he had not gone far. I was right. A few paces distant he had halted in the same dubious, lingering way. "Hallo!" I said.

He turned towards me in the like awkward fashion, but with neither astonishment nor concern.

"Come up and take a drink with me before you go," I said, "if you're not in a hurry. I'm alone here, and since I HAVE turned out I don't see why we mightn't have a smoke and a talk together."

"I dursn't."

I looked up at the six feet of strength before me and repeated wonderingly, "Dare not?"

"SHE wouldn't like it." He made a movement with his right shoulder towards the extension.

"Who?"

"Miss Karline."

"Nonsense!" I said. "She isn't in the cabin,—you won't see HER. Come along." He hesitated, although from what I could discern of his bearded face it was weakly smiling.

"Come."

He obeyed, following me not unlike Chu Chu, I fancied, with the same sense of superior size and strength and a slight whitening of the eye, as if ready to shy at any moment. At the door he "backed." Then he entered sideways. I noticed that he cleared the doorway at the top and the sides only by a hair's breadth.

By the light of the fire I could see that, in spite of his full first growth of beard, he was young,—even younger than myself,—and that he was by no means bad-looking. As he still showed signs of retreating at any moment, I took my flask and tobacco from my saddle-bags, handed them to him, pointed to the stool, and sat down myself upon the bed.

"You live near here?"

"Yes," he said a little abstractedly, as if listening for some interruption, "at Ten Mile Crossing."

"Why, that's two miles away."

"I reckon."

"Then you don't live here—on the clearing?"

"No. I b'long to the mill at 'Ten Mile.'"

"You were on your way home?"

"No," he hesitated, looking at his pipe; "I kinder meander round here at this time, when Johnson's away, to see if everything's goin' straight."

"I see—you're a friend of the family."

"'Deed no!" He stopped, laughed, looked confused, and added, apparently to his pipe, "That is, a sorter friend. Not much. SHE"—he lowered his voice as if that potential personality filled the whole cabin—"wouldn't like it."

"Then at night, when Johnson's away, you do sentry duty round the house?"

"Yes, 'sentry dooty,' that's it,"—he seemed impressed with the suggestion—"that's it! Sentry dooty. You've struck it, pardner."

"And how often is Johnson away?"

"'Bout two or three times a week on an average."

"But Miss Caroline appears to be able to take care of herself. She has no fear."

"Fear! Fear wasn't hangin' round when SHE was born!" He

paused. "No, sir. Did ye ever look into them eyes?"

I hadn't, on account of the lashes. But I didn't care to say this, and only nodded.

"There ain't the created thing livin' or dead, that she can't stand straight up to and look at."

I wondered if he had fancied she experienced any difficulty in standing up before that innocently good-humored face, but I could not resist saying:—

"Then I don't see the use of your walking four miles to look after her."

I was sorry for it the next minute, for he seemed to have awkwardly broken his pipe, and had to bend down for a long time afterwards to laboriously pick up the smallest fragments of it. At last he said, cautiously:

"Ye noticed them bits o' flannin' round the chillern's throats?"

I remembered that I had, but was uncertain whether it was intended as a preventive of cold or a child's idea of decoration. I nodded.

"That's their trouble. One night, when old Johnson had been off for three days to Coulterville, I was prowling round here and I didn't git to see no one, though there was a light burnin' in the shanty all night. The next night I was here again,—the same light twinklin', but no one about. I reckoned that was mighty queer, and I jess crep' up to the house an' listened. I heard suthin' like a little cough oncet in a while, and at times suthin' like a little moan. I didn't durst to sing out for I knew SHE wouldn't like it, but whistled keerless like, to let the chillern know I was there. But it didn't seem to take. I was jess goin' off, when—darn my skin!—if I didn't come across the bucket of water I'd fetched up from the spring THAT MORNIN', standin' there full, and NEVER TAKEN IN! When I saw that I reckoned I'd jess wade in, anyhow, and I knocked. Pooty soon the door was half opened, and I saw her eyes blazin' at me like them coals. Then SHE 'lowed I'd better 'git up and git,' and shet the door to! Then I 'lowed she might tell me what was up—through the door. Then she said, through the door, as how the chillern lay all sick with that hoss-distemper, diphthery. Then she 'lowed she'd use a doctor ef I'd fetch him. Then she 'lowed again I'd better take the baby that hadn't ketched it yet along with me, and leave it where it was safe. Then she passed out the baby through the door all wrapped up in a blankit like a papoose, and you bet I made tracks with it. I knowed thar wasn't no good going to the mill, so I let out for White's, four miles beyond, whar there was White's old mother. I told her how things were pointin', and she lent me a hoss, and I jess rounded on Doctor Green at Mountain Jim's, and had him back here afore sun-up! And then I heard she wilted,—regularly played out, you see,—for she had it all along wuss than the lot, and never let on or whimpered!"

"It was well you persisted in seeing her that night," I said, watching the rapt expression of his face. He looked up quickly, became conscious of my scrutiny, and dropped his eyes again, smiled feebly, and drawing a circle in the ashes with the broken pipe-stem, said:—

"But SHE didn't like it, though."

I suggested, a little warmly, that if she allowed her father to leave her alone at night with delicate children, she had no right to choose WHO should assist her in an emergency. It struck me afterwards that this was not very complimentary to him, and I added hastily that I wondered if she expected some young lady to be passing along the trail at midnight! But this reminded me of Johnson's style of argument, and I stopped.

"Yes," he said meekly, "and ef she didn't keer enough for herself and her brothers and sisters, she orter remember them Beazeley chillern."

"Beazeley children?" I repeated wonderingly.

"Yes; them two little ones, the size of Mirandy; they're Beazeley's."

"Who is Beazeley, and what are his children doing here?"

"Beazeley up and died at the mill, and she bedevilled her father to let her take his two young 'uns here."

"You don't mean to say that with her other work she's taking care of other people's children too?"

"Yes, and eddicatin' them."

"Educating them?"

"Yes; teachin' them to read and write and do sums. One of our loggers ketched her at it when she was keepin' tally."

We were both silent for some moments.

"I suppose you know Johnson?" I said finally.

"Not much."

"But you call here at other times than when you're

helping her?"

"Never been in the house before."

He looked slowly around him as he spoke, raising his eyes to the bare rafters above, and drawing a few long breaths, as if he were inhaling the aura of some unseen presence. He appeared so perfectly gratified and contented, and I was so impressed with this humble and silent absorption of the sacred interior, that I felt vaguely conscious that any interruption of it was a profanation, and I sat still, gazing at the dying fire. Presently he arose, stretched out his hand, shook mine warmly, said, "I reckon I'll meander along," took another long breath, this time secretly, as if conscious of my eyes, and then slouched sideways out of the house into the darkness again, where he seemed suddenly to attain his full height, and so looming, disappeared. I shut the door, went to bed, and slept soundly.

So soundly that when I awoke the sun was streaming on my bed from the open door. On the table before me my breakfast was already laid. When I had dressed and eaten it, struck by the silence, I went to the door and looked out. 'Dolphus was holding Chu Chu by the reata a few paces from the cabin.

"Where's Caroline?" I asked.

He pointed to the woods and said: "Over yon: keeping tally."

"Did she leave any message?"

"Said I was to git your mule for you."

"Anything else?"

"Yes; said you was to go."

I went, but not until I had scrawled a few words of thanks on a leaf of my notebook, which I wrapped about my last Spanish dollar, addressed it to "Miss Johnson," and laid it upon the table.

*****

It was more than a year later that in the bar-room of the Mariposa Hotel a hand was laid upon my sleeve. I looked up. It was Johnson.

He drew from his pocket a Spanish dollar. "I reckoned," he said, cheerfully, "I'd run again ye somewhar some time. My old woman told me to give ye that when I did, and say that she 'didn't keep no hotel.' But she allowed she'd keep the letter, and has spelled it out to the chillern."

Here was the opportunity I had longed for to touch Johnson's pride and affection in the brave but unprotected girl. "I want to talk to you about Miss Johnson," I said, eagerly.

"I reckon so," he said, with an exasperating smile. "Most fellers do. But she ain't Miss Johnson no more. She's married."

"Not to that big chap over from Ten Mile Mills?" I said breathlessly.

"What's the matter with HIM," said Johnson. "Ye didn't expect her to marry a nobleman, did ye?"

I said I didn't see why she shouldn't—and believed that she HAD.

THE NEW ASSISTANT AT PINE CLEARING SCHOOL

CHAPTER I

The schoolmistress of Pine Clearing was taking a last look around her schoolroom before leaving it for the day. She might have done so with pride, for the schoolroom was considered a marvel of architectural elegance by the citizens, and even to the ordinary observer was a pretty, villa-like structure, with an open cupola and overhanging roof of diamond-shaped shingles and a deep Elizabethan porch. But it was the monument of a fierce struggle between a newer civilization and a barbarism of the old days, which had resulted in the clearing away of the pines—and a few other things as incongruous to the new life and far less innocent, though no less sincere. It had cost the community fifteen thousand dollars, and the lives of two of its citizens.

Happily there was no stain of this on the clean white walls, the beautifully-written gilt texts, or the shining blackboard that had offered no record which could not be daily wiped away. And, certainly, the last person in the world to suggest any reminiscences of its belligerent foundation was the person of the schoolmistress. Mature, thin, precise,—not pretty enough to have excited Homeric feuds, nor yet so plain as to preclude certain soothing graces,—she was the widow of a poor Congregational minister, and had been expressly imported from San Francisco to squarely mark the issue between the regenerate and unregenerate life. Low-voiced, gentlewomanly, with the pallor of ill-health perhaps unduly accented by her mourning, which was still cut modishly enough to show off her spare but good figure, she was supposed to represent the model of pious, scholastic refinement. The Opposition—sullen in ditches and at the doors of saloons, or in the fields truculent as their own cattle—nevertheless had lowered their crests and buttoned their coats over their revolutionary red shirts when SHE went by.

As she was stepping from the threshold, she was suddenly confronted by a brisk business-looking man, who was about to enter. "Just in time to catch you, Mrs. Martin," he said hurriedly; then, quickly correcting his manifest familiarity, he added: "I mean, I took the liberty of running in here on my way to the stage office. That matter you spoke of is all arranged. I talked it over with the other trustees, wrote to Sam Barstow, and he's agreeable, and has sent somebody up, and," he rapidly consulted his watch, "he ought to be here now; and I'm on my way to meet him with the other trustees."

Mrs. Martin, who at once recognized her visitor as the Chairman of the School Board, received the abrupt information with the slight tremulousness, faint increase of color, and hurried breathing of a nervous woman.

"But," she said, "it was only a SUGGESTION of mine, Mr. Sperry; I really have no right to ask—I had no idea"—

"It's all right, ma'am,—never you mind. We put the case square to Barstow. We allowed that the school was getting too large for you to tackle,—I mean, you know, to superintend single-handed; and that these Pike County boys they're running in on us are a little too big and sassy for a lady like you to lasso and throw down—I mean, to sorter control—don't you see? But, bless you, Sam Barstow saw it all in a minit! He just jumped at it. I've got his letter here—hold on"—he hastily produced a letter from his pocket, glanced ever it, suddenly closed it again with embarrassed quickness, yet not so quickly but that the woman's quicker eyes were caught, and nervously fascinated by the expression "I'm d—d" in a large business hand—and said in awkward haste, "No matter about reading it now—keep you too long—but he's agreed all right, you know. Must go now—they'll be waiting. Only I thought I'd drop in a-passin', to keep you posted;" and, taking off his hat, he began to back from the porch.

"Is—is—this gentleman who is to assist me—a—a mature professional man—or a—graduate?" hesitated Mrs. Martin, with a faint smile.

"Don't really know—I reckon Sam—Mr. Barstow—fixed that all right. Must really go now;" and, still holding his hat in his hand as a polite compromise for his undignified haste, he fairly ran off.

Arrived at the stage office, he found the two other trustees awaiting him, and the still more tardy stage-coach. One, a large, smooth-faced, portly man, was the Presbyterian minister; the other, of thinner and more serious aspect, was a large mill-owner.

"I presume," said the Rev. Mr. Peaseley, slowly, "that as our good brother Barstow, in the urgency of the occasion, has, to some extent, anticipated OUR functions in engaging this assistant, he is—a—a—satisfied with his capacity?"

"Sam knows what he's about," said the mill-owner cheerfully, "and as he's regularly buckled down to the work here, and will go his bottom dollar on it, you can safely leave things to him."

"He certainly has exhibited great zeal," said the reverend gentleman patronizingly.

"Zeal," echoed Sperry enthusiastically, "zeal? Why, he runs Pine Clearing as he runs his bank and his express company in Sacramento, and he's as well posted as if he were here all the time. Why, look here;" he nudged the mill-owner secretly, and, as the minister's back was momentarily turned, pulled out the letter he had avoided reading to Mrs. Martin, and pointed to a paragraph. "I'll be d—d," said the writer, "but I'll have peace and quietness at Pine Clearing, if I have to wipe out or make over the whole Pike County gang. Draw on me for a piano if you think Mrs. Martin can work it. But don't say anything to Peaseley first, or he'll want it changed for a harmonium, and that lets us in for psalm-singing till you can't rest. Mind! I don't object to Church influence—it's a good hold!—but you must run IT with other things equal, and not let it run YOU. I've got the schoolhouse insured for thirty thousand dollars—special rates too."

The mill-owner smiled. "Sam's head is level! But," he added, "he don't say much about the new assistant he's sending."

"Only here," he says, "I reckon the man I send will do all round; for Pike County has its claims as well as Boston."

"What does that mean?" asked the mill-owner.

"I reckon he means he don't want Pine Clearing to get too high-toned any more than he wants it too low down. He's mighty square in his averages—is Sam."

Here speculation was stopped by the rapid oncoming of the stage-coach in all the impotent fury of a belated arrival. "Had to go round by Montezuma to let off Jack Hill," curtly explained the driver, as he swung himself from the box, and entered the hotel bar-room in company with the new expressman, who had evidently taken Hill's place on the box-seat. Autocratically indifferent to further inquiry, he called out cheerfully: "Come along, boys, and hear this yer last new yarn about Sam Barstow,—it's the biggest thing out." And in another moment the waiting crowd, with glasses in their hands, were eagerly listening to the repetition of the "yarn" from the new expressman, to the apparent exclusion of other matters, mundane and practical.

Thus debarred from information, the three trustees could only watch the passengers as they descended, and try to identify their expected stranger. But in vain: the bulk of the passengers they already knew, the others were ordinary miners and laborers; there was no indication of the new assistant among them. Pending further inquiry they were obliged to wait the conclusion of the expressman's humorous recital. This was evidently a performance of some artistic merit, depending upon a capital imitation of an Irishman, a German Jew, and another voice, which was universally recognized and applauded as being "Sam's style all over!" But for the presence of the minister, Sperry and the mill-owner would have joined the enthusiastic auditors, and inwardly regretted the respectable obligations of their official position.

When the story-teller had concluded amidst a general call for more drinks, Sperry approached the driver. The latter recognizing him, turned to his companion carelessly, said, "Here's one of 'em," and was going away when Sperry stopped him.

"We were expecting a young man."

"Yes," said the driver, impatiently, "and there he is, I reckon."

"We don't mean the new expressman," said the minister, smiling blandly, "but a young man who"—

"THAT ain't no new expressman," returned the driver in scornful deprecation of his interlocutor's ignorance. "He only took Hill's place from Montezuma. He's the new kid reviver and polisher for that University you're runnin' here. I say—you fellers oughter get him to tell you that story of Sam Barstow and the Chinaman. It'd limber you fellers up to hear it."

"I fear there's some extraordinary mistake here," said Mr. Peaseley, with a chilling Christian smile.

"Not a bit of it. He's got a letter from Sam for one of ye. Yere, Charley—what's your name! Com yere. Yere's all yer three bosses waiting for ye."

And the supposed expressman and late narrator of amusing stories came forward and presented his credentials as the assistant teacher of Pine Clearing.

CHAPTER II

Even the practical Mr. Sperry was taken aback. The young man before him was squarely built, with broad shoulders, and a certain air of muscular activity. But his face, although good-humored, was remarkable for offering not the slightest indication of studious preoccupation or mental training. A large mouth, light blue eyes, a square jaw, the other features being indistinctive—were immobile as a mask—except that, unlike a mask, they seemed to actually reflect the vacuity of the mood within, instead of concealing it. But as he saluted the trustees they each had the same feeling that even this expression was imported and not instinctive. His face was clean-shaven, and his hair cut so short as to suggest that a wig of some kind was necessary to give it characteristic or even ordinary human semblance. His manner, self-assured yet lacking reality, and his dress of respectable cut and material, yet worn as if it did not belong to him, completed a picture as unlike a student or schoolmaster as could be possibly conceived.

Yet there was the letter in Mr. Peaseley's hands from Barstow, introducing Mr. Charles Twing as the first assistant teacher in the Pine Clearing Free Academy!

The three men looked hopelessly at each other. An air of fatigued righteousness and a desire to be spiritually at rest from other trials pervaded Mr. Peaseley. Whether or not the young man felt the evident objection he had raised, he assumed a careless position, with his back and elbows against the bar; but even the attitude was clearly not his own.

"Are you personally known to Mr. Barstow?" asked Sperry, with a slight business asperity.

"Yes."

"That is—you are quite well acquainted with him?"

"If you'd heard me gag his style a minute ago, so that everybody here knew who it was, you'd say so."

Mr. Peaseley's eyes sought the ceiling, and rested on the hanging lamp, as if nothing short of direct providential interference could meet the occasion. Yet, as the eyes of his brother trustees were bent on him expectantly, he nerved himself to say something.

"I suppose, Mr.—Mr. Twing, you have properly understood the great—I may say, very grave, intellectual, and moral responsibilities of the work you seek to undertake—and the necessity of supporting it by EXAMPLE, by practice, by personal influence both in the school and OUT OF IT. Sir, I presume, sir, you feel that you are fully competent to undertake this?"

"I reckon HE does!"

"WHO does?"

"Sam Barstow, or he wouldn't have selected me. I presume" (with the slightest possible and almost instinctive imitation of the reverend gentleman's manner) "his head is considered level."

Mr. Peaseley withdrew his eyes from the ceiling. "I have," he said to his companions, with a pained smile, "an important choir meeting to attend this afternoon. I fear I must be excused." As he moved towards the door, the others formally following him, until out of the stranger's hearing, he added: "I wash my hands of this. After so wanton and unseemly an exhibition of utter incompetency, and even of understanding of the trust imposed upon him—upon US—MY conscience forbids me to interfere further. But the real arbiter in this matter will be—thank Heaven!—the mistress herself. You have only to confront her at once with this man. HER decision will be speedy and final. For even Mr. Barstow will not dare to force so outrageous a character upon a delicate, refined woman, in a familiar and confidential capacity."

"That's so," said Sperry eagerly; "she'll settle it. And, of course," added the mill-owner, "that will leave us out of any difficulty with Sam."

The two men returned to the hapless stranger, relieved, yet constrained by the sacrifice to which they felt they were leading him. It would be necessary, they said, to introduce him to his principal, Mrs. Martin, at once. They might still find her at the schoolhouse, distant but a few steps. They said little else, the stranger keeping up an ostentatious whistling, and becoming more and more incongruous, they thought, as they neared the pretty schoolhouse. Here they DID find Mrs. Martin, who had, naturally, lingered after the interview with Sperry.

She came forward to meet them, with the nervous shyness and slightly fastidious hesitation that was her nature. They saw, or fancied they saw, the same surprise and disappointment they had themselves experienced pass over her sensitive face, as she looked at him; they felt that their vulgar charge appeared still more outrageous by contrast with this delicate woman and her pretty, refined surroundings; but they saw that HE enjoyed it, and was even—if such a word could be applied to so self-conscious a man—more at ease in her presence!

"I reckon you and me will pull together very well, ma'am,"

he said confidently.

They looked to see her turn her back upon him; faint, or burst out crying; but she did neither, and only gazed at him quietly.

"It's a mighty pretty place you've got here—and I like it, and if WE can't run it, I don't know who can. Only just let me know WHAT you want, ma'am, and you can count on me every time."

To their profound consternation Mrs. Martin smiled faintly.

"It rests with YOU only, Mrs. Martin," said Sperry quickly and significantly. "It's YOUR say, you know; you're the only one to be considered or consulted here."

"Only just say what you want me to do," continued Twing, apparently ignoring the trustees; "pick out the style of job; give me a hint or two how to work it, or what you'd think would be the proper gag to fetch 'em, and I'm there, ma'am. It may be new at first, but I'll get at the business of it quick enough."

Mrs. Martin smiled—this time quite perceptibly—with the least little color in her cheeks and eyes. "Then you've had no experience in teaching?" she said.

"Well no."

"You are not a graduate of any college?"

"Not much."

The two trustees looked at each other. Even Mr. Peaseley had not conceived such a damning revelation.

"Well," said Mrs. Martin slowly, "perhaps Mr. Twing had better COME EARLY TOMORROW MORNING AND BEGIN."

"Begin?" gasped Mr. Sperry in breathless astonishment.

"Certainly," said Mrs. Martin in timid explanation. "If he is new to the work the sooner the better."

Mr. Sperry could only gaze blankly at his brother official. Had they heard aright? Was this the recklessness of nervous excitement in a woman of delicate health, or had the impostor cast some glamour upon her? Or was she frightened of Sam Barstow and afraid to reject his candidate? The last thought was an inspiration. He drew her quickly aside. "One moment, Mrs. Martin! You said to me an hour ago that you didn't intend to have asked Mr. Barstow to send you an assistant. I hope that, merely because he HAS done so, you don't feel obliged to accept this man against your better judgment?"

"Oh no," said Mrs. Martin quietly.

The case seemed hopeless. And Sperry had the miserable conviction that by having insisted upon Mrs. Martin's judgment being final they had estopped their own right to object. But how could they have foreseen her extraordinary taste? He, however, roused himself for a last appeal.

"Mrs. Martin," he said in a lower voice, "I ought to tell you that the Reverend Mr. Peaseley strongly doubts the competency of that young man."

"Didn't Mr. Barstow make a selection at your request?" asked Mrs. Martin, with a faint little nervous cough.

"Yes—but"—

"Then his competency only concerns ME—and I don't see what Mr. Peaseley has to say about it."

Could he believe his senses? There was a decided flush in the woman's pale face, and the first note of independence and asperity in her voice.

That night, in the privacy of his conjugal chamber, Mr. Sperry relieved his mind to another of the enigmatical sex,—the stout Southwestern partner of his joys and troubles. But the result was equally unsatisfactory. "Well, Abner," said the lady, "I never could see, for all your men's praises of Mrs. Martin, what that feller can see in HER to like!"

CHAPTER III

Mrs. Martin was early at the schoolhouse the next morning, yet not so early but that she discovered that the new assistant had been there before her. This was shown in some rearrangement of the school seats and benches. They were placed so as to form a horseshoe before her desk, and at the further extremity of this semicircle was a chair evidently for himself. She was a little nettled at his premature action, although admitting the utility of the change, but she was still more annoyed at his absence at such a moment. It was nearly the school hour when he appeared, to her surprise, marshaling a file of some of the smaller children whom he had evidently picked up en route, and who were, to her greater surprise, apparently on the best of terms with him. "Thought I'd better rake 'em in, introduce myself to 'em, and get 'em to know me before school begins. Excuse me," he went on hastily, "but I've a lot more coming up, and I'd better make myself square with them OUTSIDE." But Mrs. Martin had apparently developed a certain degree of stiffness since their evening's interview.

"It seems to me quite as important, Mr. Twing," she said drily, "that you should first learn some of your own duties, which I came here early to teach you."

"Not at all," he said cheerfully. "Today I take my seat, as I've arranged it, you see, over there with them, and watch 'em go through the motions. One rehearsal's enough for ME. At the same time, I can chip in if necessary." And before she could reply he was out of the schoolhouse again, hailing the new-comers. This was done with apparently such delight to the children and with some evidently imported expression into his smooth mask-like face, that Mrs. Martin had to content herself with watching him with equal curiosity. She was turning away with a sudden sense of forgotten dignity, when a shout of joyous, childish laughter attracted her attention to the window. The new assistant, with half a dozen small children on his square shoulders, walking with bent back and every simulation of advanced senility, was evidently personating, with the assistance of astonishingly distorted features, the ogre of a Christmas pantomime. As his eye caught hers the expression vanished, the mask-like face returned; he set the children down, and moved away. And when school began, although he marshaled them triumphantly to the very door,—with what contortion of face or simulation of character she was unable to guess,—after he had entered the schoolroom and taken his seat every vestige of his previous facial aberration was gone, and only his usual stolidity remained. In vain, as Mrs. Martin expected, the hundred delighted little eyes before her dwelt at first eagerly and hopefully upon his face, but, as she HAD NOT expected, recognizing from the blankness of his demeanor that the previous performance was intended for them exclusively, the same eager eyes were presently dropped again upon their books in simple imitation, as if he were one of themselves. Mrs. Martin breathed freely, and lessons began.

Yet she was nervously conscious, meanwhile, of a more ill-omened occurrence. This was the non-arrival of several of her oldest pupils, notably, the refractory and incorrigible Pike County contingent to whom Sperry had alluded. For the past few days they had hovered on the verge of active insubordination, and had indulged in vague mutterings which she had resolutely determined not to hear. It was, therefore, with some inward trepidations, not entirely relieved by Twing's presence, that she saw the three Mackinnons and the two Hardees slouch into the school a full hour after the lessons had begun. They did not even excuse themselves, but were proceeding with a surly and ostentatious defiance to their seats, when Mrs. Martin was obliged to look up, and—

as the eldest Hardee filed before her—to demand an explanation. The culprit addressed—a dull, heavy-looking youth of nineteen—hesitated with an air of mingled doggedness and sheepishness, and then, without replying, nudged his companion. It was evidently a preconcerted signal of rebellion, for the boy nudged stopped, and, turning a more intelligent, but equally dissatisfied, face upon the schoolmistress, began determinedly:—

"Wot's our excuse for coming an hour late? Well, we ain't got none. WE don't call it an hour late—WE don't. We call it the right time. We call it the right time for OUR lessons, for we don't allow to come here to sing hymns with babbies. We don't want to know 'where, oh where, are the Hebrew children?' They ain't nothin' to us Americans. And we don't want any more Daniels in the Lions' Den played off on us. We have enough of 'em in Sunday-school. We ain't hankerin' much for grammar and dictionary hogwash, and we don't want no Boston parts o' speech rung in on us the first thing in the mo'nin'. We ain't Boston—we're Pike County—WE are. We reckon to do our sums, and our figgerin', and our sale and barter, and our interest tables and weights and measures when the time comes, and our geograffy when it's on, and our readin' and writin' and the American Constitution in reg'lar hours, and then we calkilate to git up and git afore the po'try and the Boston airs and graces come round. That's our rights and what our fathers pay school taxes for, and we want 'em."

He stopped, looking less towards the schoolmistress than to his companions, for whom perhaps, after the schoolboy fashion, this attitude was taken. Mrs. Martin sat, quite white and self-contained, with her eyes fixed on the frayed rim of the rebel's straw hat which he still kept on his head. Then she said quietly:—

"Take off your hat, sir."

The boy did not move.

"He can't," said a voice cheerfully.

It was the new assistant. The whole school faced rapidly towards him. The rebel leader and his followers, who had not noticed him before, stared at the interrupter, who did not, however, seem to exhibit any of the authority of office, but rather the comment and criticism of one of themselves. "Wot you mean?" asked the boy indignantly.

"I mean you can't take off your hat because you've got some things stowed away in it you don't want seen," said Twing, with an immovable face.

"Wot things?" exclaimed the boy angrily. Then suddenly recollecting himself, he added, "Go along! You can't fool me! Think you'll make me take off my hat—don't you?"

"Well," said Twing, advancing to the side of the rebel, "look here then!" With a dexterous movement and a slight struggle from the boy, he lifted the hat. A half-dozen apples, a bird's nest, two birds' eggs, and a fluttering half-fledged bird fell from it. A wave of delight and astonishment ran along the benches, a blank look of hopeless bewilderment settled upon the boy's face, and the gravity of the situation disappeared forever in the irrepressible burst of laughter, in which even his brother rebels joined. The smallest child who had been half-frightened, half-fascinated by the bold, bad, heroic attitude of the mutineer, was quick to see the ridiculousness of that figure crowned with cheap schoolboy plunder. The eloquent protest of his wrongs was lost in the ludicrous appearance of the protester. Even Mrs. Martin felt that nothing she could say at that moment could lift the rebellion into seriousness again. But Twing was evidently not satisfied.

"Beg Mrs. Martin's pardon, and say you were foolin' with the boys," he said in a low voice.

The discomfited rebel hesitated.

"Say it, or I'll SHOW WHAT YOU'VE GOT IN YOUR POCKETS!" said Twing in a terribly significant aside.

The boy mumbled an apology to Mrs. Martin, scrambled in a blank, hopeless way to his seat, and the brief rebellion ignominiously ended. But two things struck Mrs. Martin as peculiar. She overheard the culprit say, with bated breath and evident sincerity, to his comrades: "Hadn't nothing in my hat, anyway!" and one of the infant class was heard to complain, in a deeply-injured way, that the bird's nest was HIS, and had been "stoled" from his desk. And there still remained the fact for which Twing's undoubted fascination over the children had somewhat prepared her—that at recess the malcontents—one and all—seemed to have forgiven the man who had overcome them, and gathered round him with unmistakable interest. All this, however, did not blind her to the serious intent of the rebellion, or of Twing's unaccountable assumption of her prerogative. While he was still romping with the children she called him in.

"I must remind you," she said, with a slight nervous asperity, "that this outrageous conduct of Tom Hardee was evidently deliberated and prepared by the others, and cannot end in this way."

He looked at her with a face so exasperatingly expressionless that she could have slapped it as if it had belonged to one of the older scholars, and said,—"But it HAS ended. It's a dead frost."

"I don't know what you mean; and I must remind you also that in this school we neither teach nor learn slang."

His immobile face changed for an instant to a look of such decided admiration that she felt her color rise; but he wiped his expression away with his hand as if it had been some artificial make-up, and said awkwardly, but earnestly:—

"Excuse me—won't you? But, look here, Mrs. Martin, I found out early this morning, when I was squaring myself with the other children, that there was this row hangin' on—in fact, that there was a sort of idea that Pike County wasn't having a fair show—excuse me—in the running of the school, and that Peaseley and Barstow were a little too much on in every scene. In fact, you see, it was just what Tom said."

"This is insufferable," said Mrs. Martin, her eyes growing darker as her cheeks grew red. "They shall go home to their parents, and tell them from me"—

"That they're all mistaken—excuse me—but that's just what THEY'RE GOIN' TO DO. I tell you, Mrs. Martin, their little game's busted—I beg pardon—but it's all over. You'll have no more trouble with them."

"And you think that just because you found Tom had something in his hat, and exposed him?" said Mrs. Martin scornfully.

"Tom HADN'T anything in his hat," said Twing, wiping his mouth slowly.

"Nothing?" repeated Mrs. Martin.

"No."

"But I SAW you take the things out."

"That was only a TRICK! He had nothing except what I had up my sleeve, and forced on him. He knew it, and that frightened him, and made him look like a fool, and so bursted up his conspiracy. There's nothin' boys are more afraid of than ridicule, or the man or boy that make 'em ridiculous."

"I won't ask you if you call this FAIR to the boy, Mr. Twing?" said Mrs. Martin hotly; "but is this your idea of discipline?"

"I call it fair, because Tom knew it was some kind of a trick, and wasn't deceived. I call it discipline if it made him do what was right afterwards, and makes him afraid or unwilling to do anything to offend me or you again. He likes me none the worse for giving him a chance of being laughed out of a thing instead of being DRIVEN out of it. And," he added, with awkward earnestness, "if you'll just leave all this to ME, and only consider me here to take this sort of work which ain't a lady's—off your hands, we'll just strike our own line between the Peaseleys and Pike County—and run this school in spite of both."

A little mollified, a good deal puzzled, and perhaps more influenced by the man's manner than she had imagined, Mrs. Martin said nothing, but let the day pass without dismissing the offenders. And on returning home that evening she was considerably surprised to receive her landlady's extravagant congratulations on the advent of her new assistant. "And they do say, Mrs. Martin," continued that lady enthusiastically, "that your just setting your foot down square on that Peaseley and that Barstow, BOTH OF 'EM—and choosing your own assistant yourself—a plain young fellow with no frills and fancies, but one that you could set about making all the changes you like, was just the biggest thing you ever did for Pine Clearing."

"And—they—consider him quite—competent?" said Mrs. Martin, with timid color and hesitating audacity.

"Competent! You ask my Johnny."

Nevertheless, Mrs. Martin was somewhat formally early at the schoolhouse the next morning. "Perhaps," she said, with an odd mixture of dignity and timidity, "we'd better, before school commences, go over the lessons for the day."

"I HAVE," he said quickly. "I told you ONE rehearsal was enough for me."

"You mean you have looked over them?"

"Got 'em by heart. Letter perfect. Want to hear me? Listen."

She did. He had actually committed to memory, and without a lapse, the entire text of rules, questions, answers, and examples of the lessons for the day.

CHAPTER IV

Before a month had passed, Mr. Twing's success was secure and established. So were a few of the changes he had quietly instituted. The devotional singing and Scripture reading which had excited the discontent of the Pike County children and their parents was not discontinued, but half an hour before recess was given up to some secular choruses, patriotic or topical, in which the little ones under Twing's really wonderful practical tuition exhibited such quick and pleasing proficiency, that a certain negro minstrel camp-meeting song attained sufficient popularity to be lifted by general accord to promotion to the devotional exercises, where it eventually ousted the objectionable "Hebrew children" on the question of melody alone. Grammar was still taught at Pine Clearing School in spite of the Hardees and Mackinnons, but Twing had managed to import into the cognate exercises of recitation a wonderful degree of enthusiasm and excellence. Dialectical Pike County, that had refused to recognize the governing powers of the nominative case, nevertheless came out strong in classical elocution, and Tom Hardee, who had delivered his ungrammatical protest on behalf of Pike County, was no less strong, if more elegant, in his impeachment of Warren Hastings as Edmund Burke, with the equal sanction of his parents. The trustees, Sperry and Jackson, had marveled, but were glad enough to accept the popular verdict—only Mr. Peaseley still retained an attitude of martyr-like forbearance and fatigued toleration towards the new assistant and his changes. As to Mrs. Martin, she seemed to accept the work of Mr. Twing after his own definition of it—as of a masculine quality ill-suited to a lady's tastes and inclinations; but it was noticeable that while she had at first repelled any criticism of him whatever, she had lately been given to explaining his position to her friends, and had spoken of him with somewhat labored and ostentatious patronage. Yet when they were alone together she frankly found him very amusing, and his presumption and vulgarity so clearly unintentional that it no longer offended her. They were good friends without having any confidences beyond the duties of the school; she had asked no further explanation of the fact that he had been selected by Mr. Barstow without reference to any special antecedent training. What his actual antecedents were she had never cared to know, nor he apparently to reveal; that he had been engaged in some other occupations of superior or inferior quality would not have been remarkable in a community where the principal lawyer had been a soldier, and the miller a doctor. The fact that he admired her was plain enough to HER; that it pleased her, but carried with it no ulterior thought or responsibility, might have been equally clear to others. Perhaps it was so to HIM.

Howbeit, this easy mutual intercourse was one day interrupted by what seemed a trifling incident. The piano, which Mr. Barstow had promised, duly made its appearance in the schoolhouse, to the delight of the scholars and the gentle satisfaction of Mrs. Martin, who, in addition to the rudimentary musical instruction of the younger girls, occasionally played upon it herself in a prim, refined, and conscientious fashion. To this, when she was alone after school hours, she sometimes added a faint, colorless voice of limited range and gentlewomanly expression. It was on one of these occasions that Twing, becoming an accidental auditor of this chaste, sad piping, was not only permitted to remain to hear the end of a love song of strictly guarded passion in the subjunctive mood, but at the close was invited to try his hand—a quick, if not a cultivated one—at the instrument. He did so. Like her, he added his voice. Like hers, it was a love song. But there the similitude ended. Negro in dialect, illiterate in construction, idiotic in passion, and presumably addressed to the "Rose of Alabama," in the very extravagance of its childish infatuation it might have been a mockery of the schoolmistress's song but for one tremendous fact! In unrestrained feeling, pathetic yearning, and exquisite tenderness of expression, it was unmistakably and appallingly personal and sincere. It was true the lips spoken of were "lubly," the eyes alluded to were like "lightenin' bugs," but from the voice and gestures of the singer Mrs. Martin confusedly felt that they were intended for HERS, and even the refrain that "she dressed so neat and looked so sweet" was glaringly allusive to her own modish mourning. Alternately flushing and paling, with a hysteric smile hovering round her small reserved mouth, the unfortunate gentlewoman was fain to turn to the window to keep her countenance until it was concluded. She did not ask him to repeat it, nor did she again subject herself to this palpable serenade, but a few days afterwards, as she was idly striking the keys in the interval of a music lesson, one of her little pupils broke out, "Why, Mrs. Martin, if yo ain't a pickin' out that pow'ful pretty tune that Mr. Twing sings!"

Nevertheless, when Twing, a week or two later, suggested that he might sing the same song as a solo at a certain performance to be given by the school children in aid of a local charity, she drily intimated that it was hardly of a character to suit the entertainment. "But," she added, more gently, "you recite so well; why not give a recitation?"

He looked at her with questioning and troubled eyes,—the one expression he seemed to have lately acquired. "But that would be IN PUBLIC! There'll be a lot of people there," he said doubtfully.

A little amused at this first apparent sign of a want of confidence in himself, she said, with a reassuring smile, "So much the better,—you do it really too well to have it thrown away entirely on children."

"Do YOU wish it?" he said suddenly.

Somewhat confused, but more irritated by his abruptness, she replied, "Why not?" But when the day came, and before a crowded audience, in which there was a fair sprinkling of strangers, she regretted her rash suggestion. For when the pupils had gone through certain calisthenic exercises—admirably taught and arranged by him—and "spoken their pieces," he arose, and, fixing his eyes on her, began Othello's defense before the Duke and Council. Here, as on the previous occasion, she felt herself personally alluded to in his account of his wooing. Desdemona, for some occult reason, vicariously appeared for her in the unwarrantable picture of his passion, and to this was added the absurd consciousness which she could not put aside that the audience, following with enthusiasm his really strong declamation, was also following his suggestion and adopting it. Yet she was also conscious, and, as she thought, as inconsistently, of being pleased and even proud of his success. At the conclusion the applause was general, and a voice added with husky admiration and familiarity:—

"Brayvo, Johnny Walker!"

Twing's face became suddenly white as a Pierrot mask. There was a dead silence, in which the voice continued, "Give us 'Sugar in the Gourd,' Johnny."

A few hisses, and cries of "Hush!" "Put him out!" followed. Mrs. Martin raised her eyes quickly to where her assistant had stood bowing his thanks a moment before. He was gone!

More concerned than she cared to confess, vaguely fearful that she was in some way connected with his abrupt withdrawal, and perhaps a little remorseful that she had allowed her personal feelings to interfere with her frank recognition of his triumph, she turned back to the schoolroom, after the little performers and their audience had departed, in the hope that he might return. It was getting late, the nearly level rays of the sun were lying on the empty benches at the lower end of the room, but the desk where she sat with its lid raised was in deep shadow. Suddenly she heard his voice in a rear hall, but it was accompanied by another's,—the same voice which had interrupted the applause. Before she could either withdraw, or make herself known, the two men had entered the room, and were passing slowly through it. She understood at once that Twing had slipped out into a janitor's room in the rear, where he had evidently forced an interview and explanation from his interrupter, and now had been waiting for the audience to disperse before emerging by the front door. They had evidently overlooked her in the shadow.

"But," said the stranger, as if following an aggrieved line of apology, "if Barstow knew who you were, and what you'd done, and still thought you good enough to rastle round here and square up them Pike County fellers and them kids—what in thunder do you care if the others DO find you out, as long as Barstow sticks to you?"

"I've told you why, Dick," returned Twing gloomily.

"Oh, the schoolma'am!"

"Yes, she's a saint, an angel. More than that—she's a lady, Dick, to the tip of her fingers, who knows nothing of the world outside a parson's study. She took me on trust—without a word—when the trustees hung back and stared. She's never asked me about myself, and now when she knows who and what I have been—she'll loathe me!"

"But look here, Jim," said the stranger anxiously. "I'll say it's all a lie. I'll come here and apologize to you afore HER, and say I took you for somebody else. I'll"—

"It's too late," said Twing moodily.

"And what'll you do?"

"Leave here."

They had reached the door together. To Mrs. Martin's terror, as the stranger passed out, Twing, instead of following him as she expected, said "Good-night," and gloomily re-entered the schoolroom. Here he paused a moment, and then throwing himself on one of the benches, dropped his head upon a desk with his face buried in his hands—like a very schoolboy.

What passed through Mrs. Martin's mind I know not. For a moment she sat erect and rigid at her desk. Then she slipped quietly down, and, softly as one of the last shadows cast by the dying sun, glided across the floor to where he sat.

"Mrs. Martin," he said, starting to his feet.

"I have heard all," she said faintly. "I couldn't help it. I was here when you came in. But I want to tell you that I am content to know you only as you seem to be,—as I have always found you here,—strong and loyal to a duty laid upon you by those who had a full knowledge of all you had been."

"Did you? Do you know what I have been?"

Mrs. Martin looked frightened, trembled a moment, and, recovering herself with an effort, said gently, "I know nothing of your past."

"Nothing?" he repeated, with a mirthless attempt at laughter, and a quick breath. "Not that I've been a—a—mountebank, a variety actor—a clown, you know, for the amusement of the lowest, at twenty-five cents a ticket. That I'm 'Johnny Walker,' the song and dance man—the all-round man—selected by Mr. Barstow to teach these boors a lesson as to what they wanted!"

She looked at him a moment—timidly, yet thoughtfully. "Then you are an actor—a person who simulates what he does not feel?"

"Yes."

"And all the time you have been here you have been acting the schoolmaster—playing a part—for—for Mr. Barstow?"

"Yes."

"Always?"

"Yes."

The color came softly to her face again, and her voice was very low. "And when you sang to me that day, and when you looked at me—as you did—an hour or two ago—while you were entertaining—you were—only—acting?"

Mr. Twing's answer was not known, but it must have been a full and complete one, for it was quite dark when he left the schoolroom—NOT for the last time—with its mistress on his arm.

IN A PIONEER RESTAURANT

CHAPTER I

There was probably no earthly reason why the "Poco Mas o Menos" Club of San Francisco should have ever existed, or why its five harmless, indistinctive members should not have met and dined together as ordinary individuals. Still less was there any justification for the gratuitous opinion which obtained, that it was bold, bad, and brilliant. Looking back upon it over a quarter of a century and half a globe, I confess I cannot recall a single witticism, audacity, or humorous characteristic that belonged to it. Yet there was no doubt that we were thought to be extremely critical and satirical, and I am inclined to think we honestly believed it. To take our seats on Wednesdays and Saturdays at a specially reserved table at the restaurant we patronized, to be conscious of being observed by the other guests, and of our waiter confidentially imparting our fame to strangers behind the shaken-out folds of a napkin, and of knowing that the faintest indication of merriment from our table thrilled the other guests with anticipatory smiles, was, I am firmly convinced, all that we ever did to justify our reputations. Nor, strictly speaking, were we remarkable as individuals; an assistant editor, a lawyer, a young army quartermaster, a bank clerk and a mining secretary—we could not separately challenge any special social or literary distinction. Yet I am satisfied that the very name of our Club—a common Spanish colloquialism, literally meaning "a little more or less," and adopted in Californian slang to express an unknown quantity—was supposed to be replete with deep and convulsing humor.

My impression is that our extravagant reputation, and, indeed, our continued existence as a Club, was due solely to the proprietor of the restaurant and two of his waiters, and that we were actually "run" by them. When the suggestion of our meeting regularly there was first broached to the proprietor—a German of slow but deep emotions—he received it with a "So" of such impressive satisfaction that it might have been the beginning of our vainglory. From that moment he became at once our patron and our devoted slave. To linger near our table once or twice during dinner with an air of respectful vacuity,—as of one who knew himself too well to be guilty of the presumption of attempting to understand our brilliancy,—to wear a certain parental pride and unconsciousness in our fame, and yet to never go further in seeming to comprehend it than to obligingly translate the name of the Club as "a leedle more and nod quide so much" —was to him sufficient happiness. That he ever experienced any business profit from the custom of the Club, or its advertisement, may be greatly doubted; on the contrary, that a few plain customers, nettled at our self-satisfaction, might have resented his favoritism seemed more probable. Equally vague, disinterested, and loyal was the attachment of the two waiters,—one an Italian, faintly reminiscent of better days and possibly superior extraction; the other a rough but kindly Western man, who might have taken this menial position from temporary stress of circumstances, yet who continued in it from sheer dominance of habit and some feebleness of will. They both vied with each other to please us. It may have been they considered their attendance upon a reputed intellectual company less degrading than ministering to the purely animal and silent wants of the average customers. It may have been that they were attracted by our general youthfulness. Indeed, I am inclined to think that they themselves were much more distinctive and interesting than any members of the Club, and it is to introduce THEM that I venture to recall so much of its history.

A few months after our advent at the restaurant, one evening, Joe Tallant, the mining secretary, one of our liveliest members, was observed to be awkward and distrait during dinner, forgetting even to offer the usual gratuity to the Italian waiter who handed him his hat, although he stared at him with an imbecile smile. As we chanced to leave the restaurant together, I was rallying him upon his abstraction, when to my surprise he said gravely: "Look here, one of two things has got to happen: either we must change our restaurant or I'm going to resign."

"Why?"

"Well, to make matters clear, I'm obliged to tell you something that in our business we usually keep a secret. About three weeks ago I had a notice to transfer twenty feet of Gold Hill to a fellow named 'Tournelli.' Well, Tournelli happened to call for it himself, and who the devil do you suppose Tournelli was? Why our Italian waiter. I was regularly startled, and so was he. But business is business; so I passed him over the stock and said nothing—nor did he—neither there nor here. Day before yesterday he had thirty feet more transferred to him, and sold out."

"Well?" I said impatiently.

"Well," repeated Tallant indignantly. "Gold Hill's worth six hundred dollars a foot. That's eighteen thousand dollars cash.

And a man who's good enough for that much money is too good to wait upon me. Fancy a man who could pay my whole year's salary with five feet of stock slinging hash to ME. Fancy YOU tipping him with a quarter!"

"But if HE don't mind it—and prefers to continue a waiter—why should YOU care? And WE'RE not supposed to know."

"That's just it," groaned Tallant. "That's just where the sell comes in. Think how he must chuckle over us! No, sir! There's nothing aristocratic about me; but, by thunder, if I can't eat my dinner, and feel I am as good as the man who waits on me, I'll resign from the Club."

After endeavoring to point out to him the folly of such a proceeding, I finally suggested that we should take the other members of our Club into our confidence, and abide by their decision; to which he agreed. But, to his chagrin, the others, far from participating in his delicacy, seemed to enjoy Tournelli's unexpected wealth with a vicarious satisfaction and increase of dignity as if we were personally responsible for it. Although it had been unanimously agreed that we should make no allusions, jocose or serious, to him, nor betray any knowledge of it before him, I am afraid our attitude at the next dinner was singularly artificial. A nervous expectancy when he approached us, and a certain restraint during his presence, a disposition to check any discussion of shares or "strikes" in mining lest he should think it personal, an avoidance of unnecessary or trifling "orders," and a singular patience in awaiting their execution when given; a vague hovering between sympathetic respect and the other extreme of indifferent bluntness in our requests, tended, I think, to make that meal far from exhilarating. Indeed, the unusual depression affected the unfortunate cause of it, who added to our confusion by increased solicitude of service and—as if fearful of some fault, or having incurred our disfavor—by a deprecatory and exaggerated humility that in our sensitive state seemed like the keenest irony. At last, evidently interpreting our constraint before him into a desire to be alone, he retired to the door of a distant pantry, whence he surveyed us with dark and sorrowful Southern eyes. Tallant, who in this general embarrassment had been imperfectly served, and had eaten nothing, here felt his grievance reach its climax, and in a sudden outbreak of recklessness he roared out, "Hi, waiter—you, Tournelli. He may," he added, turning darkly to us, "buy up enough stock to control the board and dismiss ME; but, by thunder, if it costs me my place, I'm going to have some more chicken!"

It was probably this sensitiveness that kept us from questioning him, even indirectly, and perhaps led us into the wildest surmises. He was acting secretly for a brotherhood or society of waiters; he was a silent partner of his German employer; he was a disguised Italian stockbroker, gaining "points" from the unguarded conversation of "operating" customers; he was a political refugee with capital; he was a fugitive Sicilian bandit, investing his ill-gotten gains in California; he was a dissipated young nobleman, following some amorous intrigue across the ocean, and acting as his own Figaro or Leporello. I think a majority of us favored the latter hypothesis, possibly because we were young, and his appearance gave it color. His thin black mustaches and dark eyes, we felt, were Tuscan and aristocratic; at least, they were like the baritone who played those parts, and HE ought to know. Yet nothing could be more exemplary and fastidious than his conduct towards the few lady frequenters of the "Poodle Dog" restaurant, who, I regret to say, were not puritanically reserved or conventual in manner.

But an unexpected circumstance presently changed and divided our interest. It was alleged by Clay, the assistant editor, that entering the restaurant one evening he saw the back and tails of a coat that seemed familiar to him half-filling a doorway leading to the restaurant kitchen. It was unmistakably the figure of one of our Club members,—the young lawyer,—Jack Manners. But what was he doing there? While the Editor was still gazing after him, he suddenly disappeared, as if some one had warned him that he was observed. As he did not reappear, when Tournelli entered from the kitchen a few moments later, the Editor called him and asked for his fellow-member. To his surprise the Italian answered, with every appearance of truthfulness, that he had not seen Mr. Manners at all! The Editor was staggered; but as he chanced, some hours later, to meet Manners, he playfully rallied him on his mysterious conference with the Italian. Manners replied briefly that he had had no interview whatever with Tournelli, and changed the subject quickly. The mystery—as we persisted in believing it—was heightened when another member deposed that he had seen "Tom," the Western waiter, coming from Manners's office. As Manners had volunteered no infor-mation of this, we felt that we could not without indelicacy ask him if Tom was a client, or a messenger from Tournelli. The only result was that our Club dinner was even more constrained than before. Not only was "Tom" now invested with a dark importance, but it was evident that the harmony of the Club was destroyed by these singular secret relations of two of its members with their employes.

It chanced that one morning, arriving from a delayed journey, I dropped into the restaurant. It was that slack hour between the lingering breakfast and coming luncheon when the tables are partly stripped and unknown doors, opened for ventilation, reveal the distant kitchen, and a mingled flavor of cold coffee-grounds and lukewarm soups hangs heavy on the air. To this cheerlessness was added a gusty rain without, that filmed the panes of the windows and doors, and veiled from the passer-by the usual tempting display of snowy cloths and china.

As I seemed to be the only customer at that hour, I selected a table by the window for distraction. Tom had taken my order; the other waiters, including Tournelli, were absent, with the exception of a solitary German, who, in the interlude of perfunctory trifling with the casters, gazed at me with that abstracted irresponsibility which one waiter assumes towards another's customer. Even the proprietor had deserted his desk at the counter. It seemed to be a favorable opportunity to get some information from Tom.

But he anticipated me. When he had dealt a certain number of dishes around me, as if they were cards and he was telling my fortune, he leaned over the table and said, with interrogating confidence:—

"I reckon you call that Mr. Manners of yours a good lawyer?"

We were very loyal to each other in the Club, and I replied with youthful enthusiasm that he was considered one of the most promising at the bar. And, remembering Tournelli, I added confidently that whoever engaged him to look after their property interests had secured a treasure.

"But is he good in criminal cases—before a police court, for instance?" continued Tom.

I believed—I don't know on what grounds—that Manners was good in insurance and admiralty law, and that he looked upon criminal practice as low; but I answered briskly—though a trifle startled—that as a criminal lawyer he was perfect.

"He could advise a man, who had a row hanging on, how to

steer clear of being up for murder—eh?"

I trusted, with a desperate attempt at jocosity, that neither he nor Tournelli had been doing anything to require Manners's services in that way.

"It would be too late, THEN," said Tom, coolly, "and ANYBODY could tell a man what he ought to have done, or how to make the best of what he had done; but the smart thing in a lawyer would be to give a chap points BEFOREHAND, and sorter tell him how far he could go, and yet keep inside the law. How he might goad a fellow to draw on him, and then plug him—eh?"

I looked up quickly. There was nothing in his ordinary, good-humored, but not very strong face to suggest that he himself was the subject of this hypothetical case. If he were speaking for Tournelli, the Italian certainly was not to be congratulated on his ambassador's prudence; and, above all, Manners was to be warned of the interpretation which might be put upon his counsels, and disseminated thus publicly. As I was thinking what to say, he moved away, but suddenly returned again.

"What made you think Tournelli had been up to anything?" he asked sharply.

"Nothing," I answered; "I only thought you and he, being friends"—

"You mean we're both waiters in the same restaurant. Well, I don't know him any better than I know that chap over there," pointing to the other waiter. "He's a Greaser or an Italian, and, I reckon, goes with his kind."

Why had we not thought of this before? Nothing would be

more natural than that the rich and imperious Tournelli should be exclusive, and have no confidences with his enforced associates. And it was evident that Tom had noticed it and was jealous.

"I suppose he's rather a swell, isn't he?" I suggested tentatively.

A faint smile passed over Tom's face. It was partly cynical and partly suggestive of that amused toleration of our youthful credulity which seemed to be a part of that discomposing patronage that everybody extended to the Club. As he said nothing, I continued encouragingly:—

"Because a man's a waiter, it doesn't follow that he's always been one, or always will be."

"No," said Tom, abstractedly; "but it's about as good as anything else to lie low and wait on." But here two customers entered, and he turned to them, leaving me in doubt whether to accept this as a verbal pleasantry or an admission. Only one thing seemed plain: I had certainly gained no information, and only added a darker mystery to his conference with Manners, which I determined I should ask Manners to explain.

I finished my meal in solitude. The rain was still beating drearily against the windows with an occasional accession of impulse that seemed like human impatience. Vague figures under dripping umbrellas, that hid their faces as if in premeditated disguise, hurried from the main thoroughfare. A woman in a hooded waterproof like a domino, a Mexican in a black serape, might have been stage conspirators hastening to a rendezvous. The cavernous chill and odor which I had before noted as coming from some sarcophagus of larder or oven, where "funeral baked meats" might have been kept in stock, began to oppress me. The hollow and fictitious domesticity of this common board had never before seemed so hopelessly displayed. And Tom, the waiter, his napkin twisted in his hand and his face turned with a sudden dark abstraction towards the window, appeared to be really "lying low," and waiting for something outside his avocation.

CHAPTER II

The fact that Tom did not happen to be on duty at the next Club dinner gave me an opportunity to repeat his mysterious remark to Manners, and to jokingly warn that rising young lawyer against the indiscretion of vague counsel. Manners, however, only shrugged his shoulders. "I don't know what he meant," he said carelessly; "but since he chooses to talk of his own affairs publicly, I don't mind saying that they are neither very weighty nor very dangerous. It's only the old story: the usual matrimonial infidelities that are mixed up with the Californian emigration. He leaves the regular wife behind,—fairly or unfairly, I can't say. She gets tired waiting, after the usual style, and elopes with somebody else. The Western Penelope isn't built for waiting. But she seems to have converted some of his property into cash when she skipped from St. Louis, and that's where his chief concern comes in. That's what he wanted to see me for; that's why he inveigled me into that infernal pantry of his one day to show me a plan of his property, as if that was any good."

He paused disgustedly. We all felt, I think, that Tom was some kind of an impostor, claiming the sympathies of the Club on false pretenses. Nevertheless, the Quartermaster said, "Then you didn't do anything for him—give him any advice, eh?"

"No; for the property's as much hers as his, and he hasn't got a divorce; and, as it's doubtful whether he didn't desert her first, he can't get one. He was surprised," he added, with a grim smile, "when I told him that he was obliged to support her, and was even liable for her debts. But people who are always talking of invoking the law know nothing about it." We were surprised too, although Manners was always convincing us, in some cheerful but discomposing way, that we were all daily and hourly, in our simplest acts, making ourself responsible for all sorts of liabilities and actions, and even generally preparing ourselves for arrest and imprisonment. The Quartermaster continued lazily:—

"Then you didn't give him any points about shooting?"

"No; he doesn't even know the man she went off with. It was eighteen months ago, and I don't believe he'd even know her again if he met her. But, if he isn't much of a client, we shall miss him to-night as a waiter, for the place is getting full, and there are not enough to serve."

The restaurant was, indeed, unusually crowded that evening; the more so that, the private rooms above being early occupied, some dinner parties and exclusive couples had been obliged to content themselves with the public dining saloon. A small table nearest us, usually left vacant to insure a certain seclusion to the Club, was arranged, with a deprecatory apology from the proprietor, for one of those couples, a man and woman. The man was a well-known speculator,—cool, yet reckless and pleasure-loving; the woman, good-looking, picturesquely attractive, self-conscious, and self-possessed. Our propinquity was evidently neither novel nor discomposing. As she settled her skirts in her place, her bright, dark eyes swept our table with a frank, almost childish, familiarity. The younger members of the Club quite unconsciously pulled up their collars and settled their neckties; the elders as unconsciously raised their voices slightly, and somewhat arranged their sentences. Alas! the simplicity and unaffectedness of the Club were again invaded.

Suddenly there was a crash, the breaking of glass, and an exclamation. Tournelli, no doubt disorganized by the unusual hurry, on his way to our table had dropped his tray, impartially distributed a plate of asparagus over an adjoining table, and, flushed and nervous, yet with an affectation of studied calmness, was pouring the sauce into the young Quartermaster's plate, in spite of his languid protests. At any other time we would have laughed, but there was something in the exaggerated agitation of the Italian that checked our mirth. Why should he be so upset by a trifling accident? He could afford to pay for the breakage; he would laugh at dismissal. Was it the sensitiveness of a refined nature, or—he was young and good-looking—was he disconcerted by the fact that our handsome neighbor had witnessed his awkwardness? But she was not laughing, and, as far as I could see, was intently regarding the bill of fare.

"Waiter!" called her companion, hailing Tournelli. "Here!" The Italian, with a face now distinctly white, leaned over the table, adjusting the glasses, but did not reply.

"Waiter!" repeated the stranger, sharply. Tournelli's face twitched, then became set as a mask; but he did not move. The stranger leaned forward and pulled his apron from behind. Tournelli started with flashing eyes, and turned swiftly round. But the Quartermaster's hand had closed on his wrist.

"That's my knife, Tournelli."

The knife dropped from the Italian's fingers.

"Better see WHAT he wants. It may not be THAT," said the young officer, coolly but kindly.

Tournelli turned impatiently towards the stranger. We alone had witnessed this incident, and were watching him breathlessly. Yet what bade fair a moment ago to be a tragedy, seemed now to halt grotesquely. For Tournelli, throwing open his linen jacket with a melodramatic gesture, tapped his breast, and with flashing eyes and suppressed accents said, "Sare; you wantah me? Look—I am herre!"

The speculator leaned back in his chair in good-humored astonishment. The lady's black eyes, without looking at Tournelli, glanced backward round the room, and slipped along our table, with half-defiant unconcern; and then she uttered a short hysterical laugh.

"Ah! ze lady—madame—ze signora—eh—she wantah me?" continued Tournelli, leaning on the table with compressed fingers, and glaring at her. "Perhaps SHE wantah Tournelli—eh?"

"Well, you might bring some with the soup," blandly replied her escort, who seemed to enjoy the Italian's excitement as a national eccentricity; "but hurry up and set the table, will you?"

Then followed, on the authority of the Editor, who understood Italian, a singular scene. Secure, apparently, in his belief that his language was generally uncomprehended, Tournelli brought a decanter, and, setting it on the table, said, "Traitress!" in an intense whisper. This was followed by the cruets, which he put down with the exclamation, "Perjured fiend!" Two glasses, placed on either side of her, carried the word "Apostate!" to her ear; and three knives and forks, rattling more than was necessary, and laid crosswise before her plate, were accompanied with "Tremble, wanton!" Then, as he pulled the tablecloth straight, and ostentatiously concealed a wine-stain with a clean napkin, scarcely whiter than his lips, he articulated under his breath: "Let him beware! he goes not hence alive! I will slice his craven heart—thus—and thou shalt see it." He turned quickly to a side table and brought back a spoon. "And THIS is why I have not found you;" another spoon, "For THIS you have disappeared;" a purely perfunctory polishing of her fork, "For HIM, bah!" an equally unnecessary wiping of her glass, "Blood of God!"—more wiping—"It will end! Yes"—general wiping and a final flourish over the whole table with a napkin—"I go, but at the door I shall await you both."

She had not spoken yet, nor even lifted her eyes. When she did so, however, she raised them level with his, showed all her white teeth—they were small and cruel-looking—and said smilingly in his own dialect:—

"Thief!"

Tournelli halted, rigid.

"You're talking his lingo, eh?" said her escort good-humoredly.

"Yes."

"Well—tell him to bustle around and be a little livelier with the dinner, won't you? This is only skirmishing."

"You hear," she continued to Tournelli in a perfectly even voice; "or shall it be a policeman, and a charge of stealing?"

"Stealing!" gasped Tournelli. "YOU say stealing!"

"Yes—ten thousand dollars. You are well disguised here, my little fellow; it is a good business—yours. Keep it while you can."

I think he would have sprung upon her there and then, but that the Quartermaster, who was nearest him, and had been intently watching his face, made a scarcely perceptible movement as if ready to anticipate him. He caught the officer's eye; caught, I think, in ours the revelation that he had been understood, drew back with a sidelong, sinuous movement, and disappeared in the passage to the kitchen.

I believe we all breathed more freely, although the situation was still full enough of impending possibilities to prevent peaceful enjoyment of our dinner. As the Editor finished his hurried translation, it was suggested that we ought to warn the unsuspecting escort of Tournelli's threats. But it was pointed out that this would be betraying the woman, and that Jo Hays (her companion) was fully able to take care of himself. "Besides," said the Editor, aggrievedly, "you fellows only think of YOURSELVES, and you don't understand the first principles of journalism. Do you suppose I'm going to do anything to spoil a half-column of leaded brevier copy—from an eye-witness, too? No; it's a square enough fight as it stands. We must look out for the woman, and not let Tournelli get an unfair drop on Hays. That is, if the whole thing isn't a bluff."

But the Italian did not return. Whether he had incontinently fled, or was nursing his wrath in the kitchen, or already fulfilling his threat of waiting on the pavement outside the restaurant, we could not guess. Another waiter appeared with the dinners they had ordered. A momentary thrill of excitement passed over us at the possibility that Tournelli had poisoned their soup; but it presently lapsed, as we saw the couple partaking of it comfortably, and chatting with apparent unconcern. Was the scene we had just witnessed only a piece of Southern exaggeration? Was the woman a creature devoid of nerves or feeling of any kind; or was she simply a consummate actress? Yet she was clearly not acting, for in the intervals of conversation, and even while talking, her dark eyes wandered carelessly around the room, with the easy self-confidence of a pretty woman. We were beginning to talk of something else, when the Editor said suddenly, in a suppressed voice:

"Hullo! What's the matter now?"

The woman had risen, and was hurriedly throwing her cloak over her shoulders. But it was HER face that was now ashen and agitated, and we could see that her hands were trembling. Her escort was assisting her, but was evidently as astonished as ourselves. "Perhaps," he suggested hopefully, "if you wait a minute it will pass off."

"No, no," she gasped, still hurriedly wrestling with her cloak. "Don't you see I'm suffocating here—I want air. You can follow!" She began to move off, her face turned fixedly in the direction of the door. We instinctively looked there—perhaps for Tournelli. There was no one. Nevertheless, the Editor and Quartermaster had half-risen from their seats.

"Helloo!" said Manners suddenly. "There's Tom just come in. Call him!"

Tom, evidently recalled from his brief furlough by the proprietor on account of the press of custom, had just made his appearance from the kitchen.

"Tom, where's Tournelli?" asked the Lawyer hurriedly, but following the retreating woman with his eyes.

"Skipped, they say. Somebody insulted him," said Tom curtly.

"You didn't see him hanging round outside, eh? Swearing vengeance?" asked the Editor.

"No," said Tom scornfully.

The woman had reached the door, and darted out of it as her escort paused a moment at the counter to throw down a coin. Yet in that moment she had hurried before him through the passage into the street. I turned breathlessly to the window. For an instant her face, white as a phantom's, appeared pressed rigidly against the heavy plate-glass, her eyes staring with a horrible fascination back into the room—I even imagined at us. Perhaps, as it was evident that Tournelli was not with her, she fancied he was still here; perhaps she had mistaken Tom for him! However, her escort quickly rejoined her; their shadows passed the window together—they were gone.

Then a pistol-shot broke the quiet of the street.

The Editor and Quartermaster rose and ran to the door. Manners rose also, but lingered long enough to whisper to me, "Don't lose sight of Tom," and followed them. But to my momentary surprise no one else moved. I had forgotten, in the previous excitement, that in those days a pistol-shot was not unusual enough to attract attention. A few raised their heads at the sound of running feet on the pavement, and the flitting of black shadows past the windows. Tom had not stirred, but, napkin in hand, and eyes fixed on vacancy, was standing, as I had seen him once before, in an attitude of listless expectation.

In a few minutes Manners returned. I thought he glanced oddly at Tom, who was still lingering in attendance, and I even fancied he talked to us ostentatiously for his benefit. "Yes, it was a row of Tournelli's. He was waiting at the corner; had rushed at Hays with a knife, but had been met with a derringer-shot through his hat. The lady, who, it seems, was only a chance steamer acquaintance of Hays', thought the attack must have been meant for HER, as she had recognized in the Italian a man who had stolen from her divorced husband in the States, two years ago, and was a fugitive from justice. At least that was the explanation given by Hays, for the woman had fainted and been driven off to her hotel by the Quartermaster, and Tournelli had escaped. But the Editor was on his track. You didn't notice that lady, Tom, did you?"

Tom came out of an abstracted study, and said: "No, she had her back to me all the time."

Manners regarded him steadily for a moment without speaking, but in a way that I could not help thinking was much more embarrassing to the bystanders than to him. When we rose to leave, as he placed his usual gratuity into Tom's hand, he said carelessly, "You might drop into my office to-morrow if you have anything to tell ME."

"I haven't," said Tom quietly.

"Then I may have something to tell YOU."

Tom nodded, and turned away to his duties. The Mining Secretary and myself could scarcely wait to reach the street before we turned eagerly on Manners.

"Well?"

"Well; the woman you saw was Tom's runaway wife, and Tournelli the man she ran away with."

"And Tom knew it?"

"Can't say."

"And you mean to say that all this while Tom never suspected HIM, and even did not recognize HER just now?"

Manners lifted his hat and passed his fingers through his hair meditatively. "Ask me something easier, gentlemen."

A TREASURE OF THE GALLEON

Her father's house was nearly a mile from the sea, but the breath of it was always strong at the windows and doors in the early morning, and when there were heavy "south-westers" blowing in the winter, the wind brought the sharp sting of sand to her cheek, and the rain an odd taste of salt to her lips. On this particular December afternoon, however, as she stood in the doorway, it seemed to be singularly calm; the southwest trades blew but faintly, and scarcely broke the crests of the long Pacific swell that lazily rose and fell on the beach, which only a slanting copse of scrub-oak and willow hid from the cottage. Nevertheless, she knew this league-long strip of shining sand much better, it is to be feared, than the scanty flower-garden, arid and stunted by its contiguity. It had been her playground when she first came there, a motherless girl of twelve, and she had helped her father gather its scattered driftwood—as the fortunes of the Millers were not above accepting these occasional offerings of their lordly neighbor.

"I wouldn't go far to-day, Jenny," said her father, as the girl stepped from the threshold. "I don't trust the weather at this season; and besides you had better be looking over your wardrobe for the Christmas Eve party at Sol. Catlin's."

"Why, father, you don't intend to go to that man's?" said the girl, looking up with a troubled face.

"Lawyer Miller," as he was called by his few neighbors, looked slightly embarrassed. "Why not?" he asked in a faintly irritated tone.

"Why not? Why, father, you know how vulgar and conceited he is,—how everybody here truckles to him!"

"Very likely; he's a very superior man of his kind,—a kind they understand here, too,—a great trapper, hunter, and pioneer."

"But I don't believe in his trapping, hunting, and pioneering," said the girl, petulantly. "I believe it's all as hollow and boisterous as himself. It's no more real, or what one thinks it should be, than he is. And he dares to patronize you—you, father, an educated man and a gentleman!"

"Say rather an unsuccessful lawyer who was fool enough to believe that buying a ranch could make him a farmer," returned her father, but half jestingly. "I only wish I was as good at my trade as he is."

"But you never liked him,—you always used to ignore him; you've changed, father"—She stopped suddenly, for her recollection of her father's quiet superiority and easy independence when he first came there was in such marked contrast to his late careless and weak concession to the rude life around them, that she felt a pang of vague degradation, which she feared her voice might betray.

"Very well! Do as you like," he replied, with affected carelessness; "only I thought, as we cannot afford to go elsewhere this Christmas, it might be well for us to take what we could find here."

"Take what we could find here!" It was so unlike him—he who had always been so strong in preserving their little domestic refinements in their rude surroundings, that their poverty had never seemed mean, nor their seclusion ignoble. She turned away to conceal her indignant color. She could share the household work with a squaw and Chinaman, she could fetch wood and water. Catlin had patronizingly seen her doing it, but to dance to his vulgar piping—never!

She was not long in reaching the sands that now lay before her, warm, sweet-scented from short beach grass, stretching to a dim rocky promontory, and absolutely untrod by any foot but her own. It was this virginity of seclusion that had been charming to her girlhood; fenced in between the impenetrable hedge of scrub-oaks on the one side, and the lifting green walls of breakers tipped with chevaux de frise of white foam on the other, she had known a perfect security for her sports and fancies that had captivated her town-bred instincts and native fastidiousness. A few white-winged sea-birds, as proud, reserved, and maiden-like as herself, had been her only companions. And it was now the custodian of her secret,—a secret as innocent and childlike as her previous youthful fancies,—but still a secret known only to herself.

One day she had come upon the rotting ribs of a wreck on the beach. Its distance from the tide line, its position, and its deep imbedding of sand, showed that it was of ancient origin. An omnivorous reader of all that pertained to the history of California, Jenny had in fancy often sailed the seas in one of those mysterious treasure-ships that had skirted the coast in bygone days, and she at once settled in her mind that her discovery was none other than a castaway Philippine galleon. Partly from her reserve, and partly from a suddenly conceived plan, she determined to keep its existence unknown to her father, as careful inquiry on her part had found it was equally unknown to the neighbors. For this shy, imaginative young girl of eighteen had convinced herself that it might still contain a part of its old treasure. She would dig for it herself, without telling anybody. If she failed, no one would know it; if she were successful, she would surprise her father and perhaps retrieve their fortune by less vulgar means than their present toil. Thanks to the secluded locality and the fact that she was known to spend her leisure moments in wandering there, she could work without suspicion. Secretly conveying a shovel and a few tools to the spot the next day, she set about her prodigious task. As the upper works were gone, and the galleon not large, in three weeks, working an hour or two each day, she had made a deep excavation in the stern. She had found many curious things,—the flotsam and jetsam of previous storms,—but as yet, it is perhaps needless to say, not the treasure.

To-day she was filled with the vague hope of making her discovery before Christmas Day. To have been able to take her father something on that day—if only a few old coins—the fruit of her own unsuspected labor and intuition—not the result of vulgar barter or menial wage—would have been complete happiness. It was perhaps a somewhat visionary expectation for an educated girl of eighteen, but I am writing of a young Californian girl, who had lived in the fierce glamour of treasure-hunting, and in whose sensitive individuality some of its subtle poison had been instilled. Howbeit, to-day she found nothing. She was sadly hiding her pick and shovel, as was her custom, when she discovered the fresh track of an alien foot in the sand. Robinson Crusoe was not more astounded at the savage footprint than Jenny Miller at this damning proof of the invasion of her sacred territory. The footprints came from and returned to the copse of shrubs. Some one might have seen her at work!

But a singular change in the weather, overlooked in her

excitement, here forced itself upon her. A light film over sea and sky, lifted only by fitful gusts of wind, seemed to have suddenly thickened until it became an opaque vault, narrowing in circumference as the wind increased. The promontory behind her disappeared, as if swallowed up, the distance before her seemed to contract; the ocean at her side, the color of dull pewter, vanished in a sheet of slanting rain, and by the time she reached the house, half running, half carried along by the quartering force of the wind, a full gale was blowing.

It blew all the evening, reaching a climax and fury at past midnight that was remembered for many years along that coast. In the midst of it they heard the booming of cannon, and then the voices of neighbors in the road. "There was," said the voices, "a big steamer ashore just afore the house." They dressed quickly and ran out.

Hugging the edge of the copse to breathe and evade the fury of the wind, they struggled to the sands. At first, looking out to sea, the girl saw nothing but foam. But, following the direction of a neighbor's arm, for in that wild tumult man alone seemed speechless, she saw directly before her, so close upon her that she could have thrown a pebble on board, the high bows of a ship. Indeed, its very nearness gave her the feeling that it was already saved, and its occasional heavy roll to leeward, drunken, helpless, ludicrous, but never awful, brought a hysteric laugh to her lips. But when a livid blue light, lit in the swinging top, showed a number of black objects clinging to bulwarks and rigging, and the sea, with languid, heavy cruelty, pushing rather than beating them away, one by one, she knew that Death was there.

The neighbors, her father with the others, had been running hopelessly to and fro, or cowering in groups against the copse, when suddenly they uttered a cry—their first—of joyful welcome. And with that shout, the man she most despised and hated, Sol. Catlin, mounted on a "calico" mustang, as outrageous and bizarre as himself, dashed among them.

In another moment, what had been fear, bewilderment, and hesitation was changed to courage, confidence, and action. The men pressed eagerly around him, and as eagerly dispersed under his quick command. Galloping at his heels was a team with the whale-boat, brought from the river, miles away. He was here, there, and everywhere; catching the line thrown by the rocket from the ship, marshaling the men to haul it in, answering the hail from those on board above the tempest, pervading everything and everybody with the fury of the storm; loud, imperious, domineering, self-asserting, all-sufficient, and successful! And when the boat was launched, the last mighty impulse came from his shoulder. He rode at the helm into the first hanging wall of foam, erect and triumphant! Dazzled, bewildered, crying and laughing, she hated him more than ever.

The boat made three trips, bringing off, with the aid of the hawser, all but the sailors she had seen perish before her own eyes. The passengers,—they were few,—the captain and officers, found refuge in her father's house, and were loud in their praises of Sol. Catlin. But in that grateful chorus a single gloomy voice arose, the voice of a wealthy and troubled passenger. "I will give," he said, "five thousand dollars to the man who brings me a box of securities I left in my stateroom." Every eye turned instinctively to Sol.; he answered only those of Jenny's. "Say ten thousand, and if the dod-blasted hulk holds together two hours longer I'll do it, d—n me! You hear me! My name's Sol. Catlin, and when I say a thing, by G-d, I do it." Jenny's disgust here reached its climax. The hero of a night of undoubted energy and courage had blotted it out in a single moment of native vanity and vulgar avarice.

He was gone; not only two hours, but daylight had come and they were eagerly seeking him, when he returned among them, dripping and—empty-handed. He had reached the ship, he said, with another; found the box, and trusted himself alone with it to the sea. But in the surf he had to abandon it to save himself. It had perhaps drifted ashore, and might be found; for himself, he abandoned his claim to the reward. Had he looked abashed or mortified, Jenny felt that she might have relented, but the braggart was as all-satisfied, as confident and boastful as ever. Nevertheless, as his eye seemed to seek hers, she was constrained, in mere politeness, to add her own to her father's condolences. "I suppose," she hesitated, in passing him, "that this is a mere nothing to you after all that you did last night that was really great and unselfish."

"Were you never disappointed, Miss?" he said, with exasperating abruptness.

A quick consciousness of her own thankless labor on the galleon, and a terrible idea that he might have some suspicion of, and perhaps the least suggestion that she might have been disappointed in him, brought a faint color to her cheek. But she replied with dignity:—

"I really couldn't say. But certainly," she added, with a new-found pertness, "you don't look it."

"Nor do you, Miss," was his idiotic answer.

A few hours later, alarmed at what she had heard of the inroads of the sea, which had risen higher than ever known to the oldest settler, and perhaps mindful of yesterday's footprints, she sought her old secluded haunt. The wreck was still there, but the sea had reached it. The excavation between its gaunt ribs was filled with drift and the seaweed carried there by the surges and entrapped in its meshes. And there, too, caught as in a net, lay the wooden box of securities Sol. Catlin had abandoned to the sea.

This is the story as it was told to me. The singularity of coincidences has challenged some speculation. Jenny insisted at the time upon sharing the full reward with Catlin, but local critics have pointed out that from subsequent events this proved nothing. For she had married him!

OUT OF A PIONEER'S TRUNK

It was a slightly cynical, but fairly good-humored crowd that had gathered before a warehouse on Long Wharf in San Francisco one afternoon in the summer of '51. Although the occasion was an auction, the bidders' chances more than usually hazardous, and the season and locality famous for reckless speculation, there was scarcely any excitement among the bystanders, and a lazy, half-humorous curiosity seemed to have taken the place of any zeal for gain.

It was an auction of unclaimed trunks and boxes—the personal luggage of early emigrants—which had been left on storage in hulk or warehouse at San Francisco, while the owner was seeking his fortune in the mines. The difficulty and expense of transport, often obliging the gold-seeker to make part of his journey on foot, restricted him to the smallest impedimenta, and that of a kind not often found in the luggage of ordinary civilization. As a consequence, during the emigration of '49, he was apt on landing to avail himself of the invitation usually displayed on some of the doors of the rude hostelries on the shore: "Rest for the Weary and Storage for Trunks." In a majority of cases he never returned to claim his stored property. Enforced absence, protracted equally by good or evil fortune, accumulated the high storage charges until they usually far exceeded the actual value of the goods; sickness, further emigration, or death also reduced the number of possible claimants, and that more wonderful human frailty—absolute forgetfulness of deposited possessions—combined together to leave the bulk of the property in the custodian's hands. Under an understood agreement they were always sold at public auction after a given time. Although the contents of some of the trunks were exposed, it was found more in keeping with the public sentiment to sell the trunks LOCKED and UNOPENED. The element of curiosity was kept up from time to time by the incautious disclosures of the lucky or unlucky purchaser, and general bidding thus encouraged—except when the speculator, with the true gambling instinct, gave no indication in his face of what was drawn in this lottery. Generally, however, some suggestion in the exterior of the trunk, a label or initials; some conjectural knowledge of its former owner, or the idea that he might be secretly present in the hope of getting his property back for less than the accumulated dues, kept up the bidding and interest.

A modest-looking, well-worn portmanteau had been just put up at a small opening bid, when Harry Flint joined the crowd. The young man had arrived a week before at San Francisco friendless and penniless, and had been forced to part with his own effects to procure necessary food and lodging while looking for an employment. In the irony of fate that morning the proprietors of a dry-goods store, struck with his good looks and manners, had offered him a situation, if he could make himself more presentable to their fair clients. Harry Flint was gazing half abstractedly, half hopelessly, at the portmanteau without noticing the auctioneer's persuasive challenge. In his abstraction he was not aware that the auctioneer's assistant was also looking at him curiously, and that possibly his dejected and half-clad appearance had excited the attention of one of the cynical bystanders, who was exchanging a few words with the assistant. He was, however, recalled to himself a moment later when the portmanteau was knocked down at fifteen dollars, and considerably startled when the assistant placed it at his feet with a grim smile. "That's your property, Fowler, and I reckon you look as if you wanted it back bad."

"But—there's some mistake," stammered Flint. "I didn't bid."

"No, but Tom Flynn did for you. You see, I spotted you from the first, and told Flynn I reckoned you were one of those chaps who came back from the mines dead broke. And he up and bought your things for you—like a square man. That's Flynn's style, if he is a gambler."

"But," persisted Flint, "this never was my property. My name isn't Fowler, and I never left anything here."

The assistant looked at him with a grim, half-credulous, half-scornful smile. "Have it your own way," he said, "but I oughter tell ye, old man, that I'm the warehouse clerk, and I remember YOU. I'm here for that purpose. But as that thar valise is bought and paid for by somebody else and given to you, it's nothing more to me. Take it or leave it."

The ridiculousness of quarreling over the mere form of his good fortune here struck Flint, and, as his abrupt benefactor had as abruptly disappeared, he hurried off with his prize. Reaching his cheap lodging-house, he examined its contents. As he had surmised, it contained a full suit of clothing of the better sort, and suitable to his urban needs. There were a few articles of jewelry, which he put religiously aside. There were some letters, which seemed to be of a purely business character. There were a few daguerreotypes of pretty faces, one of which was singularly fascinating to him. But there was another, of a young man, which startled him with its marvelous resemblance to HIMSELF! In a flash of intelligence he understood it all now. It was the likeness of the former owner of the trunk, for whom the assistant had actually mistaken him! He glanced hurriedly at the envelopes of the letters. They were addressed to Shelby Fowler, the name by which the assistant had just called him. The mystery was plain now. And for the present he could fairly accept his good luck, and trust to later fortune to justify himself.

Transformed in his new garb, he left his lodgings to present himself once more to his possible employer. His way led past one of the large gambling saloons. It was yet too early to find the dry-goods trader disengaged; perhaps the consciousness of more decent, civilized garb emboldened him to mingle more freely with strangers, and he entered the saloon. He was scarcely abreast of one of the faro tables when a man suddenly leaped up with an oath and discharged a revolver full in his face. The shot missed. Before his unknown assailant could fire again the astonished Flint had closed with him, and instinctively clutched the weapon. A brief but violent struggle ensued. Flint felt his strength failing him, when suddenly a look of astonishment came into the furious eyes of his adversary, and the man's grasp mechanically relaxed. The half-freed pistol, thrown upwards by this movement, was accidentally discharged point blank into his temples, and he fell dead. No one in the crowd had stirred or interfered.

"You've done for Australian Pete this time, Mr. Fowler," said a voice at his elbow. He turned gaspingly and recognized his strange benefactor, Flynn. "I call you all to witness, gentlemen," continued the gambler, turning dictatorially to the crowd, "that this man was FIRST attacked and was UNARMED." He lifted Flint's limp and empty hands and then pointed to the dead man, who was still grasping the weapon. "Come!" He caught the half-paralyzed arm of Flint and dragged him into the street.

"But," stammered the horrified Flint, as he was borne along, "what does it all mean? What made that man attack me?"

"I reckon it was a case of shooting on sight, Mr. Fowler; but he missed it by not waiting to see if you were armed. It wasn't the square thing, and you're all right with the crowd now, whatever he might have had agin' you."

"But," protested the unhappy Flint, "I never laid eyes on the man before, and my name isn't Fowler."

Flynn halted, and dragged him in a door way. "Who the devil are you?" he asked roughly.

Briefly, passionately, almost hysterically, Flint told him his scant story. An odd expression came over the gambler's face.

"Look here," he said abruptly, "I have passed my word to the crowd yonder that you are a dead-broke miner called Fowler. I allowed that you might have had some row with that Sydney duck, Australian Pete, in the mines. That satisfied them. If I go back now, and say it's a lie, that your name ain't Fowler, and you never knew who Pete was, they'll jest pass you over to the police to deal with you, and wash their hands of it altogether. You may prove to the police who you are, and how that d—clerk mistook you, but it will give you trouble. And who is there here who knows who you really are?"

"No one," said Flint, with sudden hopelessness.

"And you say you're an orphan, and ain't got any relations livin' that you're beholden to?"

"No one."

"Then, take my advice, and BE Fowler, and stick to it! Be Fowler until Fowler turns up, and thanks you for it; for you've saved Fowler's life, as Pete would never have funked and lost his grit over Fowler as he did with you; and you've a right to his name."

He stopped, and the same odd, superstitious look came into his dark eyes.

"Don't you see what all that means? Well, I'll tell you. You're in the biggest streak of luck a man ever had. You've got the cards in your own hand! They spell 'Fowler'! Play Fowler first, last, and all the time. Good-night, and good luck, MR. FOWLER."

The next morning's journal contained an account of the justifiable killing of the notorious desperado and ex-convict, Australian Pete, by a courageous young miner by the name of Fowler. "An act of firmness and daring," said the "Pioneer," "which will go far to counteract the terrorism produced by those lawless ruffians."

In his new suit of clothes, and with this paper in his hand, Flint sought the dry-goods proprietor—the latter was satisfied and convinced. That morning Harry Flint began his career as salesman and as "Shelby Fowler."

From that day Shelby Fowler's career was one of uninterrupted prosperity. Within the year he became a partner. The same miraculous fortune followed other ventures later. He was mill owner, mine owner, bank director—a millionaire! He was popular, the reputation of his brief achievement over the desperado kept him secure from the attack of envy and rivalry. He never was confronted by the real Fowler. There was no danger of exposure by others—the one custodian of his secret, Tom Flynn, died in Nevada the year following. He had quite forgotten his youthful past, and even the more recent lucky portmanteau; remembered nothing, perhaps, but the pretty face of the daguerreotype that had fascinated him. There seemed to be no reason why he should not live and die as Shelby Fowler.

His business a year later took him to Europe. He was entering a train at one of the great railway stations of London, when the porter, who had just deposited his port-manteau in a compartment, reappeared at the window followed by a young lady in mourning.

"Beg pardon, sir, but I handed you the wrong portmanteau. That belongs to this young lady. This is yours."

Flint glanced at the portmanteau on the seat before him. It certainly was not his, although it bore the initials "S. F." He was mechanically handing it back to the porter, when his eyes fell on the young lady's face. For an instant he stood petrified. It was the face of the daguerreotype. "I beg pardon," he stammered, "but are these your initials?" She hesitated, perhaps it was the abruptness of the question, but he saw she looked confused.

"No. A friend's."

She disappeared into another carriage, but from that moment Harry Flint knew that he had no other aim in life but to follow this clue and the beautiful girl who had dropped it. He bribed the guard at the next station, and discovered that she was going to York. On their arrival, he was ready on the platform to respectfully assist her. A few words disclosed the fact that she was a fellow-countrywoman, although residing in England, and at present on her way to join some friends at Harrogate. Her name was West. At the mention of his, he again fancied she looked disturbed.

They met again and again; the informality of his introduction was overlooked by her friends, as his assumed name was already respectably and responsibly known beyond California. He thought no more of his future. He was in love. He even dared to think it might be returned; but he felt he had no right to seek that knowledge until he had told her his real name and how he came to assume another's. He did so alone—scarcely a month after their first meeting. To his alarm, she burst into a flood of tears, and showed an agitation that seemed far beyond any apparent cause. When she had partly recovered, she said, in a low, frightened voice:—

"You are bearing MY BROTHER'S name. But it was a name that the unhappy boy had so shamefully disgraced in Australia that he abandoned it, and, as he lay upon his death-bed, the last act of his wasted life was to write an imploring letter begging me to change mine too. For the infamous companion of his crime who had first tempted, then betrayed him, had possession of all his papers and letters, many of them from ME, and was threatening to bring them to our Virginia home and expose him to our neighbors. Maddened by desperation, the miserable boy twice attempted the life of the scoundrel, and might have added that blood guiltiness to his other sins had he lived. I DID change my name to my mother's maiden one, left the country, and have lived here to escape the revelations of that desperado, should he fulfill his threat."

In a flash of recollection Flint remembered the startled look that had come into his assailant's eye after they had clinched. It was the same man who had too late realized that his antagonist was not Fowler. "Thank God! you are forever safe from any exposure from that man," he said, gravely, "and the name of Fowler has never been known in San Francisco save in all respect and honor. It is for you to take back—fearlessly and alone!"

She did—but not alone, for she shared it with her husband.

THE GHOSTS OF STUKELEY CASTLE

There should have been snow on the ground to make the picture seasonable and complete, but the Western Barbarian had lived long enough in England to know that, except in the pages of a holiday supplement, this was rarely the accompaniment of a Christmas landscape, and he cheerfully accepted, on the 24th of December, the background of a low, brooding sky, on which the delicate tracery of leafless sprays and blacker chevaux de frise of pine was faintly etched, as a consistent setting to the turrets and peacefully stacked chimneys of Stukeley Castle. Yet, even in this disastrous eclipse of color and distance, the harmonious outlines of the long, gray, irregular pile seemed to him as wonderful as ever. It still dominated the whole landscape, and, as he had often fancied, carried this subjection even to the human beings who had created it, lived in it, but which it seemed to have in some dull, senile way dozed over and forgotten. He vividly recalled the previous sunshine of an autumnal house party within its walls, where some descendants of its old castellans, encountered in long galleries or at the very door of their bedrooms, looked as alien to the house as the Barbarian himself.

For the rest it may be found described in the local guide-books, with a view of its "South Front," "West Front," and "Great Quadrangle." It was alleged to be based on an encampment of the Romans—that highly apocryphal race who seemed to have spent their time in getting up picnics on tessellated pavements, where, after hilariously emptying their pockets of their loose coin and throwing round their dishes, they instantly built a road to escape by, leaving no other record of their existence. Stow and Dugdale had recorded the date when a Norman favorite obtained the royal license to "embattle it;" it had done duty on Christmas cards with the questionable snow already referred to laid on thickly in crystal; it had been lovingly portrayed by a fair country-woman—the vivacious correspondent of the "East Machias Sentinel"—in a combination of the most delightful feminine disregard of facts with the highest feminine respect for titles. It was rich in a real and spiritual estate of tapestries, paintings, armor, legends, and ghosts. Everything the poet could wish for, and indeed some things that decent prose might have possibly wished out of it, were there.

Yet, from the day that it had been forcibly seized by a Parliamentary General, until more recently, when it had passed by the no less desperate conveyance of marriage into the hands of a Friendly Nobleman known to the Western Barbarian, it had been supposed to suggest something or other more remarkable than itself. "Few spectators," said the guide-book, "even the most unimpassioned, can stand in the courtyard and gaze upon those historic walls without feeling a thrill of awe," etc. The Western Barbarian had stood there, gazed, and felt no thrill. "The privileged guest," said the grave historian, "passing in review the lineaments of the illustrious owners of Stukeley, as he slowly paces the sombre gallery, must be conscious of emotions of no ordinary character," etc., etc. The Barbarian had been conscious of no such emotions. And it was for this reason, and believing he MIGHT experience them if left there in solitude, with no distracting or extraneous humanity around him, it had been agreed between him and the Friendly Nobleman, who had fine Barbarian instincts, that as he—the Friendly Nobleman—and his family were to spend their holidays abroad, the Barbarian should be allowed, on the eve and day of Christmas, to stay at Stukeley alone. "But," added his host, "you'll find it beastly lonely, and although I've told the housekeeper to look after you—you'd better go over to dine at Audley Friars, where there's a big party, and they know you, and it will be a deuced deal more amusing. And—er—I say—you know—you're really NOT looking out for ghosts, and that sort of thing, are you? You know you fellows don't believe in them—over there." And the Barbarian, assuring him that this was a part of his deficient emotions, it was settled then and there that he should come. And that was why, on the 24th of December, the Barbarian found himself gazing hopefully on the landscape with his portmanteau at his feet, as he drove up the avenue.

The ravens did NOT croak ominously from the battlements as he entered. And the housekeeper, although neither "stately" nor "tall," nor full of reminiscences of "his late lordship, the present Earl's father," was very sensible and practical. The Barbarian could, of course, have his choice of rooms—but—she had thought—remembering his tastes the last time, that the long blue room? Exactly! The long, low-arched room, with the faded blue tapestry, looking upon the gallery—capital! He had always liked that room. From purely negative evidence he had every reason to believe that it was the one formidable-looking room in England that Queen Elizabeth had not slept in.

When the footman had laid out his clothes, and his step grew fainter along the passage, until it was suddenly swallowed up with the closing of a red baize door in the turret staircase, like a trap in an oubliette, the whole building seemed to sink back into repose. Quiet it certainly was, but not more so, he remembered, than when the chambers on either side were filled with guests, and floating voices in the corridor were lost in those all-absorbing walls. So far, certainly, this was no new experience. It was past four. He waited for the shadows to gather. Light thickened beyond his windows; gradually the outflanking wall and part of a projecting terrace crumbled away in the darkness, as if Night were slowly reducing the castle. The figures on the tapestry in his room stood out faintly. The gallery, seen through his open door, barred with black spaces between the mullioned windows, presently became obliterated, as if invaded by a dull smoke from without. But nothing moved, nothing glimmered. Really this might become in time very stupid.

He was startled, however, while dressing, to see from his windows that the great banqueting hall was illuminated, but on coming down was amused to find his dinner served on a small table in its oaken solitude lit by the large electric chandelier—for Stukeley Castle under its present lord had all the modern improvements—shining on the tattered banners and glancing mail above him. It was evidently the house-keeper's reading of some written suggestion of her noble master. The Barbarian, in a flash of instinct, imagined the passage:—

"Humor him as a harmless lunatic; the plate is quite safe."

Declining the further offer of an illumination of the picture gallery, grand drawing-room, ball-room, and chapel, a few hours later he found himself wandering in the corridor with a single candle and a growing conviction of the hopelessness of his experiment. The castle had as yet yielded to him nothing that he had not seen before in the distraction of company and the garishness of day. It was becoming a trifle monotonous. Yet fine—exceedingly; and now that a change of wind had lifted the fog, and the full moon shone on the lower half of the pictures of the gallery, starting into the most artificial simulation of life a number of Van Dyke legs, farthingales, and fingers that would have deceived nobody, it seemed gracious, gentle, and innocent beyond expression. Wandering down the gallery, conscious of being more like a ghost than any of the painted figures, and that they might reasonably object to him, he wished he could meet the original of one of those pictured gallants and secretly compare his fingers with the copy. He remembered an embroidered pair of gloves in a cabinet and a suit of armor on the wall that, in measurement, did not seem to bear out the delicacy of the one nor the majesty of the other. It occurred to him also to satisfy a yearning he had once felt to try on a certain breastplate and steel cap that hung over an oaken settle. It will be perceived that he was getting a good deal bored. For thus caparisoned he listlessly, and, as will be seen, imprudently, allowed himself to sink back into a very modern chair, and give way to a dreamy cogitation.

What possible interest could the dead have in anything that was here? Admitting that they had any, and that it was not the LIVING, whom the Barbarian had always found most inclined to haunt the past, would not a ghost of any decided convictions object to such a collection as his descendant had gathered in this gallery? Yonder idiot in silk and steel had blunderingly and cruelly persecuted his kinsman in leather and steel only a few panels distant. Would they care to meet here? And if their human weaknesses had died with them, what would bring them here at all? And if not THEM—who then? He stopped short. The door at the lower end of the gallery had opened! Not stealthily, not noiselessly, but in an ordinary fashion, and a number of figures, dressed in the habiliments of a bygone age, came trooping in. They did not glide in nor float in, but trampled in awkwardly, clumsily, and unfamiliarly, gaping about them as they walked. At the head was apparently a steward in a kind of livery, who stopped once or twice and seemed to be pointing out and explaining certain objects in the room. A flash of indignant intelligence filled the brain of the Barbarian! It seemed absurd!—impossible!—but it was true! It was a holiday excursion party of ghosts, being shown over Stukeley Castle by a ghostly Cicerone! And as his measured, monotonous voice rose on the Christmas morning air, it could be heard that he was actually showing off, not the antiquities of the Castle, but the MODERN IMPROVEMENTS!

"This 'ere, gossips,"—the Barbarian instantly detected the fallacy of all the so-called mediaeval jargon he had read,—"is the Helectric Bell, which does away with our hold, hordinary 'orn blowin', and the hattendant waitin' in the 'all for the usual 'Without there, who waits?' which all of us was accustomed to in mortal flesh. You hobserve this button. I press it so, and it instantly rings a bell in the kitchen 'all, and shows in fair letters the name of this 'ere gallery—as we will see later. Will hany good dame or gaffer press the button? Will YOU, mistress?" said the Cicerone to a giggling, kerchief-coifed lass.

"Oi soy, Maudlin!—look out—will yer!—It's the soime old gag as them bloomin' knobs you ketched hold of when yer was 'ere las' Whitsuntide," called out the mediaeval 'Arry of the party.

"It is NOT the Galvanic-Magnetic machine in 'is lordship's library," said the Cicerone, severely, "which is a mere toy for infants, and hold-fashioned. And we have 'ere a much later invention. I open this little door, I turn this 'andle—called a switch—and, has you perceive, the gallery is hinstantly hilluminated."

There was a hoarse cry of astonishment from the assemblage. The Barbarian felt an awful thrill as this searching, insufferable light of the nineteenth century streamed suddenly upon the up-turned, vacant-eyed, and dull faces of those sightseers of the past. But there was no responsive gleam in their eyes.

"It be the sun," gasped an old woman in a gray cloak.

"Toime to rouse out, Myryan, and make the foire," said the mediaeval 'Arry. The custodian smiled with superior toleration.

"But what do 'ee want o' my old lanthorne," asked a yellow-jerkined stable boy, pointing to an old-fashioned horned lantern, tempus Edward III., "with this brave loight?"

"You know," said the custodian, with condescending familiarity, "these mortals worship what they call 'curios' and the 'antique,' and 'is lordship gave a matter of fifty pounds for that same lanthern. That's what the modern folk come 'ere to see—like as ye."

"Oi've an old three-legged stool in Whitechapel oi'll let his lordship 'ave cheap—for five quid," suggested the humorist.

"The 'prentice wight knows not that he speaks truly. For 'ere is a braver jest than 'is. Good folks, wilt please ye to examine yon coffer?" pointing to an oaken chest.

"'Tis but poor stuff, marry," said Maudlin.

"'Tis a coffer—the same being made in Wardour Street last year—'is lordship gave one hundred pounds for it. Look at these would-be worm-holes,—but they were made with an AUGER. Marry, WE know what worm-holes are!"

A ghastly grin spread over the faces of the spectral assembly as they gathered around the chest with silent laughter.

"Wilt walk 'ere and see the phonograph in the libry, made by Hedison, an Hamerican, which bottles up the voice and preserves it fresh for a hundred years? 'Tis a rare new fancy."

"Rot," said 'Arry. Then turning to the giggling Maudlin, he whispered: "Saw it las' toime. 'Is lordship got a piece o' moy moind that oi reeled off into it about this 'ere swindle. Fawney that old bloke there charging a tanner apiece to us for chaffin' a bit of a barrel."

"Have you no last new braveries to show us of the gallants and their mistresses, as you were wont?" said Maudlin to the Cicerone. "'Twas a rare show last time—the modish silk gowns and farthingales in the closets."

"But there be no company this Christmas," said the custodian, "and 'is lordship does not entertain, unless it be the new fool 'is lordship sent down 'ere to-day, who has been mopin' and moonin' in the corridors, as is ever the way of these wittol creatures when they are not heeded. He was 'ere in a rare motley of his own choosing, with which he thinks to raise a laugh, a moment ago. Ye see him not—not 'avin' the gift that belongs by right to my dread office. 'Tis a weird privilege I have—and may not be imparted to others—save"—

"Save what, good man steward? Prithee, speak?" said Marian earnestly.

"'Tis ever a shillin' extra."

There was no response. A few of the more bashful ghosts thrust their hands in their pockets and looked awkwardly another way. The Barbarian felt a momentary relief followed by a slight pang of mortified vanity. He was a little afraid of them. The price was an extortion, certainly, but surely he was worth the extra shilling!

"He has brought but little braveries of attire into the Castle," continued the Cicerone, "but I 'ave something 'ere which was found on the top of his portmanteau. I wot ye know not the use of this." To the Barbarian's intense indignation, the Cicerone produced, from under his, his (the Barbarian's) own opera hat. "Marry, what should be this? Read me this riddle! To it—and unyoke!"

A dozen vacant guesses were made as the showman held it aloft. Then with a conjuror's gesture he suddenly placed his thumbs within the rim, released the spring and extended the hat. The assembly laughed again silently as before.

"'Tis a hat," said the Cicerone, with a superior air.

"Nay," said Maudlin, "give it here." She took it curiously, examined it, and then with a sudden coquettish movement lifted it towards her own coifed head, as if to try it on. The Cicerone suddenly sprang forward with a despairing gesture to prevent her. And here the Barbarian was conscious of a more startling revelation. How and why he could not tell, but he KNEW that the putting on of that article of his own dress would affect the young girl as the assumption of the steel cap and corselet had evidently affected him, and that he would instantly become as visible to her as she and her companions had been to him. He attempted to rise, but was too late; she had evaded the Cicerone by ducking, and, facing in the direction of the Barbarian, clapped the hat on her head. He saw the swift light of consciousness, of astonishment, of sudden fear spring into her eyes! She shrieked, he started, struggled, and awoke!

But what was this! He was alone in the moonlit gallery,

certainly; the ghastly figures in their outlandish garb were gone; he was awake and in his senses, but, in this first flash of real consciousness, he could have sworn that something remained! Something terror-stricken, and retreating even then before him,—something of the world, modern,—and, even as he gazed, vanishing through the gallery door with the material flash and rustle of silk.

He walked quietly to the door. It was open. Ah! No doubt he had forgotten to shut it fast; a current of air or a sudden draught had opened it. That noise had awakened him. More than that, remembering the lightning flash of dream consciousness, it had been the CAUSE of his dream. Yet, for a few moments he listened attentively.

What might have been the dull reverberation of a closing door in the direction of the housekeeper's room, on the lower story, was all he heard. He smiled, for even that, natural as it might be, was less distinct and real than his absurd vision.

Nevertheless the next afternoon he concluded to walk over to Audley Friars for his Christmas dinner. Its hospitable master greeted him cordially.

"But do you know, my dear fellow," he said, when they were alone for a moment, "if you hadn't come by yourself I'd have sent over there for you. The fact is that A—wrote to us that you were down at Stukeley alone, ghost-hunting or something of that sort, and I'm afraid it leaked out among the young people of our party. Two of our girls—I shan't tell you which—stole over there last night to give you a start of some kind. They didn't see you at all, but, by Jove, it seems they got the biggest kind of a fright THEMSELVES, for they declare that something dreadful in armor, you know, was sitting in the gallery. Awfully good joke, wasn't it? Of course

YOU didn't see anything,—did you?"

"No," said the Barbarian, discreetly.

ABOUT THE AUTHOR

Francis Bret Harte (August 25, 1836–May 6, 1902) was an American author and poet, best remembered for his accounts of pioneering life in California.

Born in Albany, New York, Harte moved to California in 1853, later working there in a number of capacities, including miner, teacher, messenger, and journalist. He spent part of his life in the northern California coast town now known as Arcata, at the time it was just a mining camp on Humboldt Bay.

His first literary efforts, including poetry and prose, appeared in The Californian, an early literary journal edited by Charles Henry Webb. In 1868 he became editor of The Overland Monthly, another new literary magazine, but this one more in tune with the pioneering spirit of excitement in California. His story, "The Luck of Roaring Camp," appeared in the magazine's second edition, propelling Harte to nationwide fame.

As an established literary figure, he was appointed to the position of United States Consul in the town of Krefeld, Germany in 1878 and Glasgow in 1880. In 1885 he settled in London. During the thirty years he spent in Europe, he never abandoned writing, and maintained a prodigious output of stories that retained the freshness of his earlier work. He died in England in 1902.

Friedrich Kerst
Friedrich Nietzsche
Fyodor Dostoyevsky
G.A. Henty
G.K. Chesterton
Gabrielle E. Jackson
Garrett P. Serviss
Gaston Leroux
George A. Warren
George Ade
Geroge Bernard Shaw
George Cary Eggleston
George Durston
George Ebers
George Eliot
George Gissing
George MacDonald
George Meredith
George Orwell
George Sylvester Viereck
George Tucker
George W. Cable
George Wharton James
Gertrude Atherton
Gordon Casserly
Grace E. King
Grace Gallatin
Grace Greenwood
Grant Allen
Guillermo A. Sherwell
Gulielma Zollinger
Gustav Flaubert
H. A. Cody
H. B. Irving
H.C. Bailey
H. G. Wells
H. H. Munro
H. Irving Hancock
H. R. Naylor
H. Rider Haggard
H. W. C. Davis
Haldeman Julius
Hall Caine
Hamilton Wright Mabie
Hans Christian Andersen
Harold Avery
Harold McGrath
Harriet Beecher Stowe
Harry Castlemon
Harry Coghill
Harry Houidini

Hayden Carruth
Helent Hunt Jackson
Helen Nicolay
Hendrik Conscience
Hendy David Thoreau
Henri Barbusse
Henrik Ibsen
Henry Adams
Henry Ford
Henry Frost
Henry James
Henry Jones Ford
Henry Seton Merriman
Henry W Longfellow
Herbert A. Giles
Herbert Carter
Herbert N. Casson
Herman Hesse
Hildegard G. Frey
Homer
Honore De Balzac
Horace B. Day
Horace Walpole
Horatio Alger Jr.
Howard Pyle
Howard R. Garis
Hugh Lofting
Hugh Walpole
Humphry Ward
Ian Maclaren
Inez Haynes Gillmore
Irving Bacheller
Isabel Cecilia Williams
Isabel Hornibrook
Israel Abrahams
Ivan Turgenev
J.G.Austin
J. Henri Fabre
J. M. Barrie
J. M. Walsh
J. Macdonald Oxley
J. R. Miller
J. S. Fletcher
J. S. Knowles
J. Storer Clouston
J. W. Duffield
Jack London
Jacob Abbott
James Allen
James Andrews
James Baldwin

James Branch Cabell
James DeMille
James Joyce
James Lane Allen
James Lane Allen
James Oliver Curwood
James Oppenheim
James Otis
James R. Driscoll
Jane Abbott
Jane Austen
Jane L. Stewart
Janet Aldridge
Jens Peter Jacobsen
Jerome K. Jerome
Jessie Graham Flower
John Buchan
John Burroughs
John Cournos
John F. Kennedy
John Gay
John Glasworthy
John Habberton
John Joy Bell
John Kendrick Bangs
John Milton
John Philip Sousa
John Taintor Foote
Jonas Lauritz Idemil Lie
Jonathan Swift
Joseph A. Altsheler
Joseph Carey
Joseph Conrad
Joseph E. Badger Jr
Joseph Hergesheimer
Joseph Jacobs
Jules Vernes
Julian Hawthrone
Julie A Lippmann
Justin Huntly McCarthy
Kakuzo Okakura
Karle Wilson Baker
Kate Chopin
Kenneth Grahame
Kenneth McGaffey
Kate Langley Bosher
Kate Langley Bosher
Katherine Cecil Thurston
Katherine Stokes
L. A. Abbot
L. T. Meade

L. Frank Baum
Latta Griswold
Laura Dent Crane
Laura Lee Hope
Laurence Housman
Lawrence Beasley
Leo Tolstoy
Leonid Andreyev
Lewis Carroll
Lewis Sperry Chafer
Lilian Bell
Lloyd Osbourne
Louis Hughes
Louis Joseph Vance
Louis Tracy
Louisa May Alcott
Lucy Fitch Perkins
Lucy Maud Montgomery
Luther Benson
Lydia Miller Middleton
Lyndon Orr
M. Corvus
M. H. Adams
Margaret E. Sangster
Margret Howth
Margaret Vandercook
Margaret W. Hungerford
Margret Penrose
Maria Edgeworth
Maria Thompson Daviess
Mariano Azuela
Marion Polk Angellotti
Mark Overton
Mark Twain
Mary Austin
Mary Catherine Crowley
Mary Cole
Mary Hastings Bradley
Mary Roberts Rinehart
Mary Rowlandson
M. Wollstonecraft Shelley
Maud Lindsay
Max Beerbohm
Myra Kelly
Nathaniel Hawthrone
Nicolo Machiavelli
O. F. Walton
Oscar Wilde

Owen Johnson
P.G. Wodehouse
Paul and Mabel Thorne
Paul G. Tomlinson
Paul Severing
Percy Brebner
Percy Keese Fitzhugh
Peter B. Kyne
Plato
Quincy Allen
R. Derby Holmes
R. L. Stevenson
R. S. Ball
Rabindranath Tagore
Rahul Alvares
Ralph Bonehill
Ralph Henry Barbour
Ralph Victor
Ralph Waldo Emmerson
Rene Descartes
Ray Cummings
Rex Beach
Rex E. Beach
Richard Harding Davis
Richard Jefferies
Richard Le Gallienne
Robert Barr
Robert Frost
Robert Gordon Anderson
Robert L. Drake
Robert Lansing
Robert Lynd
Robert Michael Ballantyne
Robert W. Chambers
Rosa Nouchette Carey
Rudyard Kipling
Saint Augustine
Samuel B. Allison
Samuel Hopkins Adams
Sarah Bernhardt
Sarah C. Hallowell
Selma Lagerlof
Sherwood Anderson
Sigmund Freud
Standish O'Grady
Stanley Weyman
Stella Benson
Stella M. Francis

Stephen Crane
Stewart Edward White
Stijn Streuvels
Swami Abhedananda
Swami Parmananda
T. S. Ackland
T. S. Arthur
The Princess Der Ling
Thomas A. Janvier
Thomas A Kempis
Thomas Anderton
Thomas Bailey Aldrich
Thomas Bulfinch
Thomas De Quincey
Thomas Dixon
Thomas H. Huxley
Thomas Hardy
Thomas More
Thornton W. Burgess
U. S. Grant
Upton Sinclair
Valentine Williams
Various Authors
Vaughan Kester
Victor Appleton
Victor G. Durham
Victoria Cross
Virginia Woolf
Wadsworth Camp
Walter Camp
Walter Scott
Washington Irving
Wilbur Lawton
Wilkie Collins
Willa Cather
Willard F. Baker
William Dean Howells
William le Queux
W. Makepeace Thackeray
William W. Walter
William Shakespeare
Winston Churchill
Yei Theodora Ozaki
Yogi Ramacharaka
Young E. Allison
Zane Grey